"I Should Forgive, But . . ."

"I Should Forgive, But . . ."

FINDING RELEASE FROM ANGER AND BITTERNESS

Dr. Chuck LYNCH

WORD PUBLISHING

NASHVILLE

A Thomas Nelson Company

LIVING FOUNDATION MINISTRIES
611 R.D. Mize Road
Blue Springs, MO 64014

Word Publishing, Nashville, Tennessee

Library of Congress Cataloging-in-Publication Data
Lynch, Chuck, 1942–
    I should forgive, but— : finding release from anger and bitterness / Chuck Lynch.
        p.   cm.
    ISBN 0-8499-4001-X
    1. Forgiveness—Religious aspects—Christianity. 2. Pastoral counseling. I. Title.
BV4647.F55L96   1998
234'.5—dc21   98–23652
                                                                      CIP

Printed in the United States of America
8 9 0 1 2 3 4 DHC 9 8 7 6 5 4 3 2 1

*Dedicated to
a praying mom and a forgiven dad*

Contents

Foreword

Several months ago I got a real zinger, a situation that deeply hurt my feelings. A friend pulled me away from a group we were with and pointed out how I had "messed up big-time" with a mutual friend. I was stunned. My face flushed and I felt like crawling into a hole. I knew my intentions had been pure in that particular situation, but I also knew I couldn't defend my behavior without escalating the situation. So I swallowed my pride. I took the reprimand, desperately wishing I could fire back. I knew, though, that if I started talking I was capable of making the situation much worse.

I was hurt, and I experienced the grieving process for weeks. After some time, I watched my heart heal. I remain aware that these types of situations, as painful as they can be, are simply life. As Christians we may be tax-exempt in our giving, but we are not trial-exempt in our living. Every believer is going to get hurt emotionally or even physically in life. Being an author and a speaker does not stop me from hurting others or being hurt by others. I will be hurt, frustrated, and fearful again. But the same God who healed me this time will deepen me and heal my heart again.

For years I have made a practice of "unloading" my emotions each day before the sun sets. Whenever I've experienced hurt, frustration, anger, or feelings of being unsafe with someone, I've consciously chosen to forgive. Three things have motivated me to do this.

First, failure to forgive plunges me into darkness which keeps me from walking with God in His light (1 John 1:5–7). But something else happens as well: barriers start to be erected between others and myself. I have personally observed in thousands of lives around the world that the wall is usually the size of the anger in their heart. Finally, if I do not unload anger through forgiveness, I tend to resist the attempts of others to love me. In fact, I may even find myself sabotaging my most important relationships with my wife, Norma, and my kids.

I make it a practice with my own family and the staff at Today's Family to give them the gift of forgiveness daily to keep us ministering in the light as we walk in God's light. But this is not easy. Forgiveness is hard. There are many deep reasons why forgiveness is hindered from taking place. That's why I was thrilled when I read Chuck's manuscript, *"I Should Forgive, But . . ."*. He answers at least ten of the most frequently encountered roadblocks to forgiveness. As I read, names of friends and family leaped into my mind—people I knew would be greatly helped if they could work through these roadblocks to freedom. I have already sent scores of the draft copy to personal friends and national leaders.

After I read his manuscript, I called Chuck at his home on New Year's Day with one question: Would he let me mentor him through the publishing process? It is an absolute personal joy to see the book now coming to fruition. It is refreshing for me to recommend to you both a practical book and a credible author. Chuck and I have worked together in a national ministry. I have seen the fruit of his life, his ministry, and his family grow for over twenty-five years.

—Gary Smalley

Acknowledgments

Words cannot express my deep gratefulness for the support staff of Living Foundation Ministries who have laboriously translated my hieroglyphic-like handwriting onto the computer.

Betty Barlow began this mammoth task many years ago. Teresa Grindstaff volunteered many long hours of data entry work. Melissa Luppens came to my rescue during the Christmas holidays. Nadine Kenney carried the lion's share of the work through literally hundreds of pages of revisions. Patricia Maxfield added the final corrections.

Sylvia Stone, a published author and editor for a major denominational publishing house, volunteered to final edit the manuscript.

How can I begin to thank my wife, Linda, for her tireless proofreading and encouraging support that made this all possible?

I will be eternally grateful to Gary Smalley for his enthusiastic encouragement and for introducing me to Sealy M. Yates, one of the best literary agents an author could have. And heartfelt appreciation goes to Tom Thompson, Sealy's helpful associate who navigated me through many of the business and legal details of this project.

How can I thank Lee Gessner, Senior Vice President and Deputy Publisher of Word Publishing, for his leap of faith in accepting this project for publication? Ami McConnell, Senior

Editor, did a terrific job of coaching me through each detail of publication.

No project of this magnitude would be possible if it were not for Conrad and Eda Graham—they believed in us enough to make it financially possible for me to write this book.

Finally, I want to honor all of those brave men and women who gave me permission to tell their heartrending stories of how they were able to do what for them was initially impossible. They courageously moved from "I Should forgive, but . . ." to *I did forgive and am blessed*.

Preface

The hammer slammed to the concrete basement floor as I instinctively grabbed my smashed thumb. Oh, it hurt! I had missed the nail and hit the thumb. Moments later the pain gradually reduced, leaving me with a low-grade, pulsing throb.

Days later, the brilliant purple piercing through my healing thumb nail was all that was left to remnd me of that earlier excruciating pain. The body had healed. I felt better. I could use the injured hand again. I could cautiously return to my remodeling project.

Physical pain reduces as the body heals itself. But there is another pain that does not heal with time alone: emotional pain. Especially the pain of rejection, abandonment, betrayal, abuse, and a myriad other deep emotional wounds.

The number one cry from a woulded heart is for the pain to end. The heart cries, "I want it to stop hurting! I want it to just go away. I'm tired of hurting. I want to be free! I want closure."

Closure. Conflict over. Ended. Settled. Relationship restored. The proverbial hatchet buried once and for all! And yet, achieving that kind of peace requires forgiveness. Though we many know this, something inside may cry, *Yes, I know I should forgive, but* . . .

"What do I do with my anger?"

"What if I can't forgive and forget?"

"Shouldn't they have to pay for what they have done?"
"They won't even admit they did anything wrong!"
"How can I live with the losses every day?"
"I just can't let go."
"I'm afraid they'll do it again."

Or the question may be, "Where do I begin?" Or, "How can I help someone else who needs to forgive?"

A Two-Track Book

When I asked many friends, both laymen and professional counselors, to read the initial drafts of *"I Should Forgive, But . . ."*, I was frequently asked: "Was this written for people-helpers to learn how to lead others to forgiveness, or was it directed toward those who themselves need to forgive?"

My answer to both of those questions is yes. Let me explain. As a pastor-counselor, I do not focus on fixing people's problems. Instead I act as a coach and share biblical tools (truths) that individuals can use to address their own problems. It may be necessary to practice using these tools right in my office. If a couple is not accustomed to saying "I was wrong," I have them actually say it to each other at appropriate times. If they have had no experience in saying "I forgive you," I have them turn to the spouse that just admitted they were wrong and say just that: "I forgive you." Amazingly, no one ever died when they did this, even though they had rarely, if ever, said this to each other before.

I have had people tell me that they would fall over if they ever heard their mate say they were sorry. Others have said they would rather die than say it themselves. These dire predictions aside, repentance and forgiveness always bring new life to a relationship rather than death.

Why do I emphasize providing tools rather than dispensing a quick "fix" to counselees? Simple. If I solve a problem for them, without teaching them how to solve problems on their own, whenever they have another problem, they (in theory) would have to return to my office for additional help. However, if I equip them with the tools they need, they can build and maintain healthy relationships without any assistance from me. Not only that, tools are reusable. Just as the tools one uses to build a deck can be used later on to build a shed, so it is with biblical tools: They are both transferable and applicable to many areas of life.

People have assured me through the years that they appreciate this approach. Why? If they are provided with the tools they need to deal with problems in living, they will have the resources they need to help themselves and others later on. This brings us to the second reason for teaching tools to live by. I do not view people as counselees, but as trainees. Although no one comes to counseling with this perspective, we tell them early on that it is our desire that what they learn here, they will pass on to others. This concept is not new. The Apostle Paul explains, "God comforts us in all our afflictions so that we may be able [have the ability and the resource] to comfort those who are in any affliction with the comfort with which we ourselves are comforted by God" (2 Cor. 1:4).

No physical or emotional pain happens in a purposeless vacuum. One of the purposes is to prepare us to help others. One pastor asked if I would meet with a couple who were members in his church. He said he felt he was in over his head in this particular counseling situation. After agreeing to work with them, I issued an invitation to him to sit in on the sessions because he had expressed a desire to be a more effective pastor-counselor. Even with a large church and a packed schedule, he did it.

While working with the couple, I would turn to Pastor Rex and explain in front of them why I asked the questions I asked and why they answered as they did. This is exactly what I am going to do with you. You are going to sit in on many people-helping sessions with me. Often, I will give you commentary on what I am doing and why. From this you will hopefully be able to do two things: First, you will learn how to work through the hard issues of giving or receiving forgiveness. We will identify the hindrances to forgiveness and address the question of how to remove them. Second, you will learn how to help others do this for themselves.

Counseling ministry is such a vital gift from God and an effective tool to build up families in the body of Christ. I am deeply honored to serve the Lord in this area and am humbled to have you join me in this journey.

—Chuck Lynch

Chapter 1

"I Should Forgive, But..."

The phone rang and rang. I dashed over to the desk, picked it up, and answered: "Living Foundation Ministries, Chuck speaking."

"Chuck?"

The caller sounded surprised to hear my voice on the other end of the phone. He expected our receptionist.

"I can't believe I got straight through to you! I don't know what to do, Chuck."

The caller's now familiar voice changed from a startled tone to one of exasperation.

"Is this Clay?" I inquired.

"Yes. And I'm really over my head with this one, Chuck."

Clay was a young pastor, fresh out of Bible college, and a gifted young man. He was pastoring a small Midwest church which was full of big-city type problems. I had been one of his college professors in years past, and he would often call me for advice with difficult counseling problems.

"This couple I'm counseling is literally at each other's throats. I just mention the word forgiveness, and you'd think I had just thrown a can of high octane gas on a campfire—

they explode! Man! What's the big deal? You'd think I'd asked them to cut off an arm! In fact, I bet they'd rather cut off an arm than forgive. They know they sould forgive but . . . they stubbornly refuse. Why is it so hard for people to forgive? I just don't get it!"

There is not a pastor, parent, or Christian counselor who has not smashed headlong into the forgiveness impasse. Ironically, we are not referring here to people who do not have even an inkling of religious exposure. Rather, we are talking about people who have a clear understanding of what it means to be forgiven personally by God! They have experienced God's forgiveness of their sin. Unfortunately, however, that is where it ends. For them, God's forgiveness is one thing. But for them to extend it to someone who has deeply hurt them is quite another matter! They know they should forgive but bitterly refuse.

A missionary friend once quoted this couplet that I have often heard repeated:

"To live above with the saints we love, oh,
that will be glory!
But to live below with the saints we know,
that's another story."

Forgiveness lays the basic foundation for any continuing relationship. Scripture tells us that we all offend others at some time (James 3:2)—that's a given. However, forgiving others when they offend us is another matter. It's one of the hardest things we must do in order to maintain our relationships.

Learning to forgive starts early. Little Billy and Tommy get into a shoving match. Billy strikes Tommy. Tommy's wail brings a busy mother into the fray to see what has happened. Both children are wrong. Peacemaker Mom kneels down and firmly admonishes Billy to say, "I'm sorry," to which Tommy is to say, "I forgive you," and vice versa. Although she can get the boys to say the words, in reality it may take hours for them to actually be reconciled. In the adult world it may take days or months. For some, years—if ever.

The forgiveness impasse carries on generationally. The onset of adulthood does not automatically make forgiveness any easier. If anything, it only makes it harder. Why? First, because it is always easier to do in adulthood what we saw role-modeled in childhood. If children see and hear their mother and father ask for and receive forgiveness, the children will come to think that's normal. If it is rarely or never observed, then there is no pattern to follow. Secondly, although children can be stubborn, their pride is less developed. There is innocent humility. That is why Jesus referred to children as models of humility when He taught that adults would never make it into the Kingdom unless they became in heart and attitude like children (Luke 18:16–17).

As a college professor, perhaps the number one complaint I heard from collegians regarding their home life was that they rarely heard their Christian parents say, "I was wrong," "I apologize," or "Will you please forgive me?" Instead, they justified their un-Christlike behavior by blaming their outbursts on the child's offensive conduct or some outside factor. As a result, the children carried this same behavior into adulthood, and the anger and bitterness passed on to another generation.

After thirty-five years of helping people work through their problems from a biblical perspective, it is my opinion that anger and bitterness are the culprits behind eighty-five percent of all the difficult issues we deal with on a daily basis. Yet, the big surprise is that I can count on two hands (and have fingers left over!) the number of people who come to counseling with no knowledge that they need to forgive. They all know they should forgive but cannot do it. Just like the couple Pastor Clay was working with, they *knew* at the outset they needed to forgive each other. So why couldn't they? Why did it seem so impossible? What were the obstacles?

Potential failure in this regard seems to stare me in the face daily. Not necessarily in the explanation of biblical principles, but in their application. People often refuse to apply them in obedience to God's Word. And the hardest thing to get anyone to do—bar none—is to forgive.

I saw an example of this when a woman named Betty poured out her heart over her brother's preferential treatment by her dad and told how she was only tolerated and never valued, appreciated, or acknowledged—I knew we were going to have to address her bitterness and the need to release it through forgiveness. Knowing that she probably knew she needed to forgive, I skipped the "need to" issue and asked a purely academic question: "When you think of forgiveness what comes to your mind?" This is not a complicated question. At least it sounds easy. But I never cease to be amazed at the answers I receive to this question, and Betty was no exception. I have concluded that the concept of forgiveness has picked up so much unnecessary baggage, that people know they should forgive but find it hard—if not impossible—to forgive.

For years I have been on a personal journey interviewing hundreds of individuals and couples regarding the relationship between personal hurts and their ability to forgive. I have had to spend little time explaining the need to forgive. When people come to me, they usually already know they need to forgive. That's not the issue. Their problem is knowing what forgiveness actually entails and how to do it.

From observing the many cases involving the need to forgive, I've come to the conclusion that the number one roadblock to forgiveness is not stubbornness, as it appears to be on the surface, but *ignorance*—ignorance in at least two areas: First, everyone has heard of the word *forgiveness*, but few know what the word actually means. Perhaps the biggest confusion in this regard is the distinction between what it actually means to forgive, and what the results of doing so are.

For example, many say that forgiveness means "I now can stand to be around someone who has hurt me." To them, that is what forgiveness *means*. But "standing to be around someone who hurt me" is a *result* of forgiveness.

"I don't get upset anymore when I think of them" is another "definition" I hear. But again, that effect is not forgiveness—it is another result, or benefit, received *after* forgiveness has been granted.

This confusion over the *action* of forgiveness and the *results* of forgiveness is one reason forgiveness may be hard. The second reason is that there may be "peripheral" issues getting in the way. This is what Pastor Clay was experiencing with the couple he was counseling. Frequently, there are hindering issues that may be only *indirectly* related to the function of forgiveness. But ignorance of these issues and how to resolve them makes forgiveness hard, if not impossible.

Shortly, you will meet Sally. She could not forgive because she could not acknowledge the emotion of anger that would notify her that she was hurt. When you meet Andrew, you may be as surprised as I was to learn why he could not let go of his bitterness toward his physician-dad. He knew he sould forgive his dad but was not willing to do so until I addressed a separate, but related, issue first. For these friends, it was the secondary issues that made forgiveness hard. "Secondary?" To me they were, but not to them. Oftentimes I have found that what I consider to be a secondary issue can be *the* primary issue for an offended person.

"CLEAR THE DECKS"

Jesus wanted his disciples to focus totally on the Kingdom of God and on His righteousness. He could have commanded them to do it. You may say, "but He did. He said, 'Seek first His Kingdom and His righteousness' " (Matt. 6:33), and I would agree. But look at what our Lord said prior to these direct commands.

Jesus had to address his disciples' personal anxiety issues about their future security before He could get them to focus on the Kingdom. He told them, "Do not be anxious for your life, as to what you shall eat, or what you shall drink; nor for your body, as to what you shall put on." But He then challenged them: "Is not life more than food, and the body than clothing?" (Matt. 6:25). To drive the point home, He compared the Heavenly Father's provision for the birds with their personal worth to God, concluding that their worth was far greater than that of the birds (Matt. 6:26). He reminded them that, " . . . all these things the Gentiles eagerly seek." And then He addressed their deepest fears: ". . . for your Heavenly Father knows that you need all these things" (Matt. 6:32). By this He was implying that if their Heavenly Father knows their needs, out of His love and personal care for them, He would provide them. Exhibit one was the birds.

With their hindering issues of anxiety about the future addressed, Jesus was then able to challenge His disciples to "seek first His Kingdom and His righteousness." He concluded by reminding them, " . . . and all these things shall be added to you" (Matt. 6:33). He had to clear the decks of fear before he pressed them to focus on the Kingdom.

INSTANT OBEDIENCE

Jesus drew us down to the bottom line of love. "If you love Me," He declared, "you will keep My commandments" (John 14:15). And in case that was not clear, He stated it in reverse: "He who does not love Me does not keep My words" (John 14:24). Our Lord desires the same loving, obedient relationship with us that He had with His Father. "If you keep My commandments, you will abide in My love; just as I have kept My Father's commandments, and abide in His love" (John 15:10).

It is God's desire that we obey immediately. This is the ideal. Yet King David revealed an insight regarding our nature, that makes his writings helpful to many: "For He Himself knows our frame; He is mindful that we are but dust" (Ps. 103:14). God knows that there may be a distance between the command to obey and obedience. There may be issues of fear, trust, and security that need to be addressed before obedience is realized.

Our Lord was confronted by the chief priests and elders of the people. They blatantly challenged His authority in chasing out the money-changers and other merchandisers from the temple. When they did so, He turned the tables on

7

them and addressed an issue pertinent to our discussion—obedience. He told them a story about a man who had two sons. This father sent his first son to work in the family vineyard. The son immediately responded to his father's request by saying definitively, "I will sir." Then Jesus added this commentary, " . . . and he did not go" (Matt. 21:29).

The father approached the second son with the same request. He firmly responded by saying, "I will not." Then Jesus added, " . . . yet he afterward regretted it and went" (Matt. 21:30).

It is interesting to note the question Jesus then posed to these religious professionals: "Which of the two did the will of his father?" (Matt. 21:31). He did not ask which had the best attitude or displayed more respect to his father. He went straight to the bottom line—who was obedient?

This point is crucial. I know God desires His children to obey—ideally instantly. But, since He knows our frame, He demonstrates patience and mercy until obedience is accomplished. There may be obstacles we have put in front of our obedience that have to be worked through. This was exactly the case with the friends you will meet in this book. God desired each of them either to forgive or to receive forgiveness. And, for their benefit, the sooner the better. But just like the second son in our Lord's story, some processing had to precede the obedient response.

This is why Paul instructed the young minister Timothy to "preach the word; be ready in season and out of season; reprove, rebuke, exhort, with great patience and instruction" (2 Tim. 4:2). Note two important words: *patience*, which indicates time, and *instruction*, which indicates content. Both are important. It will take time to accomplish a heart and behavior change. And during that time, certain information may have to be conveyed before the end goal of obedience is accomplished.

MAKING THE LIST

As I found myself hearing repeated patterns of why people would not or could not forgive, I started keeping a list of all the reasons people either refused or found it hard to forgive. To my amazement the list was not very long. As I compiled a biblical response to each of these excuses and shared them, I was pleasantly surprised to see that at least eighty-five percent of hurting people were able to do the hardest thing they had ever done in their lives. They found the most important key to their future happiness. They were able to unlock the deadbolt of unforgiveness and walk through an open door to freedom.

Nancy, for example, had reached a roadblock. She kept saying over and over to me that she must not be able to forgive because she couldn't forget the offense. She did not realize that forgiveness and forgetting are two separate issues. For her, they were one.

Fred could not forgive because he believed his alcoholic dad should be punished for what he did. Someone had to pay. He was right. The only question was, who was going to pay and how?

Rochelle lived in fear of even being with her missionary dad who had sexually abused her. She knew she should forgive him. However, if forgiveness meant she had to be with him and jeopardize her young children in the process, no way!

Dan was a walking emotional scar. He lived daily with the memories of his abusive dad. How could Kevin ever forgive someone who so damaged him emotionally that he could barely live with the consequences of the daily reminders?

Shirley's sin carried a lot of shame. It was like a gray cloud that followed her. A well-known national speaker said she needed to forgive herself. Why couldn't she? Why didn't it work?

Death came calling at Carol's home—for her only son. Where was God when he was killed? Why did He give a son to her and then just take him? "God hurt me. I'm angry at Him and I can't forgive Him." The confusion of two major truths kept her stuck, hurt, and bitter.

I've never met anyone quite like Anne. She experienced almost every hindrance to forgiveness that I knew of. It was doubly hard for her, but she did it! How? As you will see, Anne has become a pattern of release and freedom for many.

◊

Sally's life was not working for her. Her husband was an elder in their church. She was angry but would not admit it. She was about to face the first and hardest step in forgiveness.

Chapter 2

"I'm Not Angry!"

But *I'm not angry at Carl*," Sally said as she defensively shook her head. "I'm just frustrated. I get frustrated with him and the kids, but who doesn't get frustrated once in a while?" She glanced at the floor, a little startled at her own outburst of emotion. "I'll admit that I get frustrated, but it's just an emotion. It's not like I'm raging with anger or anything like that."

I paused, looking at my notepad reflectively. The silence was deafening. I lifted my eyes slowly and looked up at Sally, hoping to express understanding and an accepting attitude. "Sally," I began, "may I share something with you that you might find helpful?"

I say this often to counselees, because I've found that although people come for counseling they may not really want to see the truth or face reality. So, I usually ask a counselee's permission to share something with them. Asking permission to share an insight opens the door of understanding while making a statement tends to close it. The reason is simple. Most adults prefer to be asked something rather than to be told something. Asking a question also opens the door of their curiosity. Even Jesus asked questions before sharing a truth or giving an instruction (Luke 9:18–20).

"Sally," I began slowly, "were you aware that every person, whether a Christian or not, experiences the hurt of emotional and physical pain?" Her eyes rolled upward in a "yeah, let's-get-this-over-with-quickly" expression.

Jesus acknowledged this to His disciples when He told them that they had peace in Him, but that while they lived in the world, they would have tribulation (John 16:33). The apostle Paul declared likewise that, "all who desire to live godly in Christ Jesus will be persecuted" (2 Tim. 3:12). And Peter, too, reminded us that Christians were actually selected by God to "suffer" (1 Pet. 2:20–21).

Sally glared, expressing her indignation. "I already know that!"

I continued, "Most people are aware of their hurts but fail to recognize that anger is an automatic emotional response to those hurts. This is true whether you are a Christian or not."

"How can that be, if anger is a work of the flesh? Anger is a sin, and Christians are not to sin if they love the Lord!"

She reeled off her assertions like a memorized catechism.

Yes, anger is listed as one of the deeds of the flesh (Gal. 5:20). But it is sin only if it is dealt with according to the flesh. It is important to remember that anger is also an automatic emotional response that needs to be acknowledged and dealt with properly and promptly. Paul expressed it this way: "Be angry, and yet do not sin; do not let the sun go down on your anger" (Eph. 4:26). In other words, when you are angry, do not sin by holding on to it for days. Process it as soon as possible, even before the day ends. Notice here again that the prohibition is not against the presence of anger, it is against failing to work through the anger in a biblical and timely fashion. Paul makes this clear later in the passage when he says that anger must "be put away from you" (Eph. 4:31). Why? Because you are the most vulnerable to the evil one when you are angry (4:27).

THE RED LIGHT OF ANGER

Years ago all cars had gauges on their dashboards instead of red lights. These gauges registered the actual temperature of the motor, the amount of oil pressure, and the amount of electricity the generator was producing. Although these gauges were indicators of some very important information, it was not long before the automakers realized three things: 1) few people were watching these gauges, 2) even fewer knew what they meant, and 3) only a fraction of drivers understood what to do with the information.

Solution? Replace the gauges with lights—red lights. These red lights were affectionately referred to as "idiot lights." Why? Because any person with even an ounce of common sense would know that if a red light came on, the car had a need. The red lights were "notifiers." They notified the driver of a need under the hood of the car.

Anger is the "red light" God uses to notify us that there is a need in our life. It is not designed to shame, but to notify of a need. Yes, I have friends that drive their cars with the red light on and ignore it. A few have even had to replace their engines because the red lights were ignored. Some even taped over the red light. One person told me that he drove with one foot on the dashboard to cover the light! You can do this. But it is usually detrimental to the car and your health to continue this practice.

So it is with your spiritual life and emotional health. Ignore the notifier of anger and there will be a high cost—not only spiritually, but mentally and physically as well. Dr. C. Everett Koop, our former U.S. Surgeon General, asserts that eighty percent of all medical illnesses seen in a physician's office are either precipitated by emotional stress—e.g., anger—or will be further worsened by emotional stressors, such as anger. Spiritually, the ensuing bitterness is bad not only in itself, it can ruin the lives of others as well (Heb. 12:15). Remember, no emotion is buried dead. It will go somewhere and come out somehow—and usually not in healthy ways. Modern psychology confirms this. Psychologists today are generally convinced that anger that is ignored or suppressed is the cause of about ninety-five percent of psychological depressions.

Another discovery will surface when you start probing into the possible presence of anger—anxiety. The fear of discovery and acknowledgment of anger is a major source of anxiety.

With those who are reluctant to acknowledge their anger, I explain that if we do not acknowledge the anger and the offense, we will not forgive it and will therefore repeat it in our own life and call it normal. If we fail to identify the offensive behavior of others and call it for what it is—sin—we will not forgive it and will reproduce it in our own lives, calling it "normal" behavior. But by identifying it, forgiving it, and releasing it, we are much less apt to reproduce it. If you excuse it in others, you will excuse it in yourself. Your children will identify with it and reproduce it in their lives generationally.

"Sally," I continued, "when it comes to anger, God gives you permission to do two things: First, you have permission even to have the normal emotional response to an offense (i.e., anger) but secondly, you have permission—in fact, an obligation—to deal with it biblically through forgiveness. God desires that you use the biblical tools (such as forgiveness) that He's provided for you to work through your anger for your good and His glory (Matt. 5:16). However, if you do not recognize the deeper hurt which anger reveals (i.e., the need to forgive), you will not see the opportunity to use His Word in a helping, healing manner." It is hard—if not impossible—to forgive if you do not acknowledge the emotion and then determine what offense brought about the emotion. You cannot forgive what you do not acknowledge. If you are at war in your heart but do not admit it to yourself, you will never forgive, bury the hatchet, and experience inner or outer peace. True, your hatchet may never strike another person, but it will decimate you on the inside.

Sally is not alone in her confused thinking in regard to the appropriateness and place of anger. Many sincere believers feel it is wrong even to have the normal emotion of anger. For some, anger is equated with "out-of-control" rage. What many Christians fail to understand is that anger has "degrees" or various "speeds." I explained it to Sally this way:

"Sally, you mentioned that you get 'peeved.' Well, did you know that when you are 'peeved,' you are angry? Yes, it may be anger that drives at only 10 m.p.h., but it is anger. Others may say they're 'agitated,' or 'irritated,' or 'frustrated.' Well, they are actually angry too! You see, 'agitation' is anger at about 15 m.p.h. 'Irritation' is anger that rides about 25 m.p.h. 'Frustration' may drive as fast as 45 m.p.h. A 'hot-temper'—manifested by yelling, screaming, and slamming of doors—speeds about 65 m.p.h. And 'out-of-control rage' floors the pedal at 80+ m.p.h. These emotions may be expressed in different 'gears' or 'speeds,' but they are all driven by the same motor of anger."

Sally flashed back to a statement her angry mother frequently made: "I'm not mad; I'm just frustrated!" Sally had translated her mother's statement into two beliefs: 1) It is not safe to admit to being angry at 65 m.p.h., but 2) you can act out anger at a lower "speed" and call it "frustration" or some other euphemism. Why? Because of the inherent shame or guilt that would spring to the surface. If you are convinced that the emotion of anger is in itself evil, you will either deny the anger or rename it with a euphemism. This explains why believers would rather lie than acknowledge their anger. I have often heard people say in a terse, defensive tone, "But I'm not angry."

Anger is the most denied or lied about emotion a person can experience. When Sally began to describe her relationship with her husband, stating she was frustrated, I interrupted, "You mean angry?"

After a few of these interruptions, she began to realize her anger and blurted out, "OK, I'm really ticked! No, I'm livid with anger. I've been angry for years—I admit it! I've been so hurt. . . ." She burst into tears. Denial was broken, and the healing process began as she acknowledged her deep pain. The first hindrance to forgiveness was removed—she acknowledged her anger. Soon she would be able to list the specific offenses and then begin the biblical process of forgiveness. If anger is the number one cause in destroying relationships, then genuine forgiveness is the number one tool in restoring relationships and burying the proverbial hatchet in peace.

THE RED FLAG OF FORGIVENESS

No medical patient will let a doctor put a cast on his arm if he does not believe it is broken. But when the doctor's

preliminary diagnosis is followed by an X-ray, clearly exposing the fracture, the patient is more willing to submit to the
cast. This willingness to process, or deal with the situation,
is not always the case with anger.

Sally finally acknowledged her deep hurt and pent-up
anger, but she was not automatically willing to deal with it
and its sources. Often, when I mention the word *forgiveness*
to a deeply hurt friend, his whole countenance changes to
adamant resistance. It is almost tantamount to waving the
proverbial red flag in front of a bull. He comes charging at
you—his two sharply-honed horns ready to gouge, at a
moment's notice, any obstacle that gets in his way—one horn
defending his anger and the other blaming the offender for
it.

This resistance to the process of forgiveness usually comes
from at least four sources. First, there is a reluctance to recall
the old hurt and to re-feel the pain. If this is the case, I point
out that the "God of all comfort" promises to comfort by
giving us hope and strength as we work through the emotional pain to forgiveness (2 Cor. 1:3–4). He is just like a car-
ing mother, who stands beside the dental chair, holding her
young son's hand as the dentist performs some painful procedure. He does not prevent the pain but makes it tolerable
as we go through it.

Second, there is the feeling that no one will understand.
In this particular situation, I have found it helpful to personally acknowledge the reality of the counselee's hurt *with*
him as he shares bits and pieces of his story with me.
Compassionately acknowledging the extent of his pain, and
validating both the appropriateness of his pain and his response
to it, gives him the freedom to admit, or accept, his feelings.
This acceptance becomes the seed bed for working through

his anger to forgiveness. By admitting the reality of his anger instead of denying it, a healthy environment is created which allows him to look more objectively at the offense and the offender, and then to see clearly how to apply the biblical process of forgiveness.

Biblical processes are the tools God gives us to establish and maintain relationships. But confusion about these tools often leads to an inaccurate concept of what biblical forgiveness is. This lack of information, or misinformation, leads to the third source of resistance to forgive; that is, the belief that anger is sin.

Sally flatly believed she was wrong to experience the human emotion of anger. One of the reasons came from her belief in the myth that the emotion of anger is wrong in itself. Again, this is contrary to the clear teaching of Scripture. Although the apostle Paul, under the inspiration of the Holy Spirit, declared, "Be angry, and yet do not sin," (Eph. 4:26), what Sally heard through years of church involvement was, "Do not sin by being angry." That is a biblical rewrite. What this verse is actually saying is: "Be angry, *but do not work it out in a sinful manner*," (yet do not sin). You have full permission by God to acknowledge the anger. The emotion of anger itself is not sinful, but the manner in which we deal with our anger may be.

Confusion over the belief that anger is automatically a sin prevented Sally from acknowledging the hurt that her anger was attempting to "notify" her of. Thus, she was not even able to get to the "I should forgive" stage and forgive those who caused the hurt.

Lack of information or misinformation regarding anger and forgiveness has kept many sincere believers locked in bitterness. Bitterness is the house that anger built. It is not a vacation condominium, but a prison. It is only as we come to understand the truth of human emotions and biblical forgiveness that we can truly use the acknowledgment of our anger as a doorway to set us free from the prison of bitterness that keeps us captive.

DOCTRINES OF MEN

Often the opinions of men regarding anger are equated with biblical doctrine when, in reality, they can be the "doctrines of demons" motivated by Satan as a scheme to confuse us (2 Cor. 2:11). Jesus confronted the Pharisees on this very issue of equating opinions of men with the doctrines of God. They had equated the teaching of the elders with Scripture. Jesus reminded them that this was not a new practice when He quoted the prophet Isaiah and applied it to them: "But in vain do they worship Me, teaching as doctrines the precepts of men" (Mark 7:7).

As I sat in my office week after week helping people to become free of past and present hurts, I began to see a pattern develop. I found that almost every difficult case of unforgiveness had at its root at least one unbiblical belief. These misbeliefs had been handed down for years, and were held to be from God when, in reality, they were precepts of men or even, a doctrine of demons (Matt. 15:9; 1 Tim. 4:1). Those who sincerely believe these untruths, or frankly lies, are also likely to find it hard, if not impossible, to forgive. But through the years many have found release from the storehouse of anger and bitterness by replacing the opinions of men with the clear truth of Scripture. God's truth does indeed set us free (John 8:32), and God gives grace only for the truth (John 1:14).

SHAME

The fourth, and final, hindrance to the process of forgiveness is the deep sense of shame or guilt that can come when the anger is acknowledged. Sally adamantly retained an appearance of emotional security by denying her anger. It was not so much that she did not know she *had* anger as it was her deep sense of shame for even *having* it.

But what does shame have to do with hindering forgiveness? Simple: Behind the emotion of shame is the emotion of fear, and this fear has three parts. The first part is the fear of discovery (i.e., I have anger). Why would Sally fear this discovery? The answer is found in the second part of fear: rejection. Her collective fear was, "If you knew [discovered] the real me [angry], you would not like me" [rejection]. This leads to the final aspect of fear—the fear of abandonment or of being alone. Apparently God knew that being alone could have negative repercussions. Just look at the creation account in Genesis 1 and 2. Each time God created something, He said "it was good." But when He saw that man was alone, He said "it is not good." This issue was the only negative thing said about the original creation. "Then the Lord God said, 'It is not good for the man to be alone, I will make him a helper suitable for him'" (Gen. 2:18).

This three-part fear system was set up in the Garden of Eden following the sin of Adam and Eve who ate of the forbidden fruit (Gen. 3:6). The first recorded emotion was, apparently, shame. As a result of their shame, they hid their nakedness from each other (Gen. 3:7).

The second emotion was fear. When they heard the sound of the Lord God walking in the garden, panic set in, and they hid themselves from the presence of God. Why? They probably reasoned that if God knew (discovered) what they had done, He would not like them, and He would reject them. When God inquired where they were, their response was not to answer where they were, but what they did and why: "I heard the sound of Thee in the garden, and I was afraid [fear] because I was naked [shame]; so I hid myself" (Gen. 3:10). Ironically, they had not had any previous experience of sin, shame, discovery, or rejection. All of this came with the introduction of sin. This sense of shame and fear of abandonment has been passed on generationally through sin. This fear of ultimate abandonment is one of the greatest fears the human race experiences. Sally, by denying her anger, tried to avoid the shame and the potential subsequent rejection.

I have heard parents shame their children when they exhibited appropriate anger. They were told they have an "attitude problem" and that they need to "get over" their bad attitude. By doing this, parents fail to address the legitimacy of the child's anger. It is important to know that when anger is equated with a bad "attitude," a child actually hears that he is bad, and that something is wrong with him because he has emotions. As he grows up he learns that whenever a natural emotion surfaces, it is to be "stuffed," or repressed, because he does not want to feel the shame of being "bad" and is therefore hindered from using the biblical tool of forgiveness.

A child should feel open to inform his parents that he is angry—not by shouting, screaming, or slamming doors— but by honestly telling them he is hurt and what he is angry about. Often, an angry child "explodes" because he has no outlet for acknowledging his anger in a healthy way. Many Christians escape the shame of being angry by using the euphemisms mentioned before. Instead of acknowledging their anger, they say, "I'm frustrated," "ticked," "peeved," or "irritated." These terms seem to be more acceptable. However, they usually side-step the acknowledgment of anger and, as a result, hinder the process of forgiveness.

Sometimes children and spouses have legitimate gripes. If they are not addressed, the hurt deepens and the anger comes out in aggressive or explosive ways—like yelling, slamming doors, or throwing things. Or, it may come out in subtle ways—like sarcasm, cynicism, or criticism. The sense of shame that has been wrongfully attached to healthy anger forces both the emotion and the person into an emotional hiding place. As a result, hearts are never healed and relationships are never restored through forgiveness. However, when a person is able to share the truth of his emotions in love—especially the normal emotion of anger—he "comes out of hiding" and is freed up to take the first step toward restoring the fractured relationship.

Sally looked up with her head slightly tilted. Her facial expression was one I have seen so frequently when an individual has just been given permission to be angry and still be accepted. It is an expression that says, "this is too good to be true." Often, in reacting to their anger, the person has said or done some sinful things in the past. These are still wrong and must be confessed (2 John 1:9). But in many cases these wrong actions are merely an outgrowth of not having had permission to acknowledge anger up front ("be angry") and to work it through in a Christlike manner ("sin not"). Giving permission to be angry early in life can avoid a lot of pain later in life. Giving Sally permission to feel legitimate anger removed that roadblock to forgiveness and cleared the way for her healing journey to begin.

"I Can't Forget!"

◊

For Nancy the vivid memories of her preacher-father's abuse continued to haunt her thoughts. This only deepened her confusion and made it hard to forgive.

Chapter 3

"I Can't Forget!"

Nancy *didn't struggle* with the emotions of anger that Sally felt, but with the memories of her father's abuse. "If I still remember," she reasoned, "I must not have forgiven him." For Nancy the forgive-and-forget philosophy was not working.

Nancy was the youngest of three daughters in a pastor's home. Her only memories of childhood were painful. There was no affection shown her. She lived in constant fear she might do something to cause a violent verbal explosion from her father. She was never allowed to express any thought or emotion of her own.

As Nancy grew older, she watched her father greet and encourage the people of his congregation with praise and approval. She longed to be one of them, rather than his daughter, so that she could receive the same love and approval. People would say to her, "Oh, it must be wonderful to be his daughter. He is such a wonderful man." She would feel sick to her stomach, but would smile and say yes. She learned at an early age to keep up the illusion of the perfect family.

Nancy's dad was the final authority on absolutely

everything, and there was no changing him. Her mother never questioned him, and was always protecting him and making sure the children did nothing to set off his anger.

One time Nancy lied to her dad and deserved to be corrected. The "correction," however, turned out to be a beating that left her bruised and battered. When it was all over she asked her mother why she did not stop him. Her mother replied, "If you hadn't lied, he wouldn't have had to punish you." Nancy felt abandoned and unprotected.

FALSE LOGIC

As I watched Nancy continue to unravel the painful past of her family, I could see the continued conflict of emotions written across her face. The feeling, "I love my parents," came into conflict with the thought, "my parents deeply hurt me."

"I think I have forgiven my dad, but I must not have, because I still remember vividly what he did to me."

I paused briefly, then gently said to Nancy, "I hope you never forget what your parents did to you."

"What are you saying? How can you be a minister of Christ and tell me that? Christ doesn't remember our sin when we confess it. We are to be like Christ, put it behind us, and never remember it again!"

Nancy was confused about some basic truths of the Bible. She had unintentionally blended many half-truths with a healthy dose of the opinions of men. She had believed a frequently held misbelief—the false "forgive-and-forget" logic that says, "If I have truly forgiven, I can forget the offense." This not only made it hard to forgive but well nigh impossible. That was the crux of her conflict. She could not forget, and thus concluded she must not have forgiven her father. Nancy failed to understand that forgiving and forgetting are two separate issues.

I told her that the reason I hoped she would never forget what her father had done to her was because God had both a temporal and an eternal purpose for her pain, and He was going to work it out for her good and His glory (Matt. 5:16). Knowing the way God created our minds, it would be virtually impossible for her to forget totally, anyway. I knew the hurt would continue as long as she expected herself to do something that was physically impossible.

THE INCREDIBLE BRAIN

I briefly explained to Nancy some incredible features of our brain as related to memory. All memories are stored in the brain by electronic impulses and by chemical transference. Messages are sent simultaneously from nerve to nerve both electronically and chemically. Memory is not a spiritual function—it's a biological function. Our brain can store at least six hundred memories a second. That would work out to about one-and-a-half trillion bits of information if we were to live seventy-five years. That is awesome when I consider that I don't even remember what I had for breakfast two days ago. My wife, Linda, is able to recall in vivid detail something that happened years ago, when I can barely recall the event itself.

Because of the way our mind works, the memories of the hurts inflicted on Nancy were permanently recorded both electronically and chemically. Forgiving does not destroy this normal physical function of the body that God designed. Christians' brains do not function any differently than non-Christians' brains. Therefore, advocates of forgive-and-forget theology need to remember that memory is a normal physical function, and not a spiritual function.

I have forgiven my own alcoholic father for abandoning his three young sons; however, I have constant reminders of those turbulent days through family photos in which his presence is conspicuously absent.

Salvation converts the spirit, not the mind (John 3:6). True, many perspectives change at the point of salvation, but not the total reasoning patterns of the mind. It has to be renewed day by day after conversion (Rom. 12:2).

GOD'S ATTRIBUTES

I asked Nancy, who grew up hearing a lot of sermons, Bible teaching, and Sunday school lessons, to tell me about some of the characteristics or attributes of God she had learned. A "what-does-this-have-to-do-with-anything?" expression appeared on her face, but she complied.

"Well, He can do anything."

"Right, and we call this the attribute of omnipotence."

"He is everywhere."

"Good, this is the attribute of omnipresence."

"I guess He even knows everything about everything."

"Great, now what do we call that attribute?"

"Omniscience."

"Now, let me ask you a simple question. How can an omniscient God forget?"

"He can't. If He did forget, He would not know everything, and God's character demands that He know everything."

"Do you believe that an omniscient God has forgotten the wrong things we have done?"

"Well, yes, if we confess our sins, He forgives our sins and remembers them no more. Even the Bible states that."

"Think for a minute, Nancy. Can the all-knowing God ever forget? Will His attribute of omniscience ever let Him forget?"

"I don't know how He does, but I know He does, because He says so in the Bible."

PROBLEM PASSAGES

Nancy had sat in on about forty-five years of preaching and teaching and was thoroughly acquainted with the Bible. Just a few of the verses that she brought up were:

Jeremiah 31:34: "Their sin I will remember no more."

Psalm 103:12: "As far as the east is from the west, so far has He removed our transgressions from us."

Micah 7:19: "He will tread our iniquities under foot. Yes, Thou wilt cast all their sin, into the depths of the sea."

Hebrews 10:17: "And their sins and their lawless deeds I will remember no more."

One of the most important tools for interpreting the Word of God is to compare a Scripture verse with other verses in the Bible. Failure to do so leads to many false interpretations and beliefs that are sincere but, unfortunately, sincerely wrong. These false beliefs, or misbeliefs, cause a great deal of emotional distress when we try to apply God's Word in ways it was never intended to be applied.

BIBLICAL SOLUTION

Many difficult disciplines of the Christian faith, such as forgiveness, can be traced to an inadequate understanding of who God is. A.W. Tozer has accurately stated, "A right concept of God is basic not only to systematic theology but to practical Christian living as well...I believe there is scarcely an error in doctrine or a failure in applying Christian ethics that cannot be traced finally to imperfect and ignoble thoughts about God" (*The Knowledge of the Holy*, p. 2).

One such conflict arises with our lack of understanding of what is true about the attributes of God. The one that was causing Nancy such difficulty was God's omniscience. She believed God could honestly forget. Nancy had to come to understand that God would be less than perfect if He did forget. That would imply God could be informed of something He forgot. As equal to the truth that God cannot lie (Heb. 6:18) is the reality that God cannot learn.

Isaiah asked some probing questions confirming this, "Who has directed the Spirit of the Lord, or as His counselor informed Him? With whom did He consult and who gave Him understanding? And who taught Him in the path of justice and taught Him knowledge, and informed Him of the way of understanding?" (Isa. 40:13–14).

The apostle Paul quoted these same words to the Roman believers after he attempted to declare "Oh, the depth of the riches both of the wisdom and knowledge of God! How unsearchable are His judgments and unfathomable His ways!" (Rom. 11:33).

In order for God to forget, He would have to be less than perfect in knowledge. This God would be less than the Most High God, the Author and Creator of the heavens and earth. When this understanding was pressed with Nancy, she more than wholeheartedly agreed. When her thinking matched the greater understanding of what is true of God, it made a significant change in her, resulting in removal of an obstacle to forgiveness.

How can we reconcile these seemingly problem passages with God's attribute of omniscience? We must remember that God uses human terminology to explain or illustrate a heavenly reality. Jesus did this with Nicodemus when attempting to explain the new birth (John 3:1–13). When Jesus asserted the need to be born again before one could enter the kingdom of God, Nicodemus thought he was going to have to somehow re-enter his mother's womb for a second birth experience. Jesus had to clarify that He was talking about being born from above by the Holy Spirit. He then proceeded to compare this phenomenon with the wind. In total exasperation, Nicodemus cried out, "How can these things be?" (John 3:9). He still could not understand that Jesus was using human illustrations to explain divine realities. And they were just that—illustrations.

"Nancy, where is the east and west in relation to our omnipresent God? King David said, 'Where can I go from Thy Spirit? Or where can I flee from Thy presence? If I ascend to heaven, Thou art there? If I make my bed in Sheol, behold, Thou art there' (Ps. 139:7–8). David couldn't go anywhere without God being there."

David pictured the concept of forgiveness accurately in the Old Testament when he said, "How blessed is the man to whom the Lord does not impute iniquity" (Ps. 32:2). Likewise, Paul described this same concept of imputation. "God was in Christ reconciling the world to Himself, not counting [imputing] their trespasses against them" (2 Cor. 5:19).

The Hebrew word which is translated "impute," and the Greek word translated as "counting" carry the same idea.

They are financial accounting terms that mean "reckon to one's account." The bill was once owed, but it has been paid; therefore, there is no balance due. These words do not imply in any sense that there was never a bill owed, just that the bill had been paid in full. The apostle Paul strongly urged Philemon to reckon Onesimus's debt to himself (see Philem. 1:18). Paul was asking that he be allowed to pay Onesimus's "debt" in full.

This concept was graphically illustrated to me one Christmas. Having been raised in Southern California, I was used to having a big barbecue for our Christmas dinner. One Christmas, with these pleasant memories in mind, our family decided to barbecue at Christmas time in Kansas City. So, we shoveled the snow off the patio and fired up the gas grill.

A month later my youngest daughter came in from playing in the snow and announced to me that she had discovered that the gas grill had been left on. Then came the bill!

Now, let's suppose that I personally take this $150 gas bill to the gas company. I walk up to the payment clerk and present my bill. As she brings up my bill on her computer screen, she says, "Yes, Mr. Lynch, your bill is $150." As I begin to write out a check to pay the bill, the manager steps up. Noticing the rather large bill, he takes three fifty-dollar bills out of his own pocket, places them on the counter, and instructs the clerk to credit the money to my account. The clerk complies, and I walk out in shock.

Now let's say a week later, as I am driving down the highway, I think I may have only dreamed that the bill had been paid. I make a quick return visit to the gas company and ask the payment clerk to pull up my account on her computer screen. She does so and says, "Mr. Lynch, I see here that your last month's bill was $150 and that it has been paid in full. Did you have any questions?"

"Oh, no," I gasp in relief, "I was just checking. Thank you." Would it be more appropriate for me to feel depressed and angry because I used to owe $150, or happy that I no longer owe any debt and ecstatic that someone else paid it? When God says He remembers our sin no more, it means He remembers it against us no more. He paid our sin bill Himself.

Let's suppose the clerk said, "I remember you, Mr. Lynch, and I don't think it was fair that the manager paid this for you. You should have to pay the bill, too."

What do you think my response would be? "I'm sorry you feel that way, but the bill will not be paid twice. It has already been paid in full." We will revisit this issue again later with Fred.

DOUBLE PAYMENT

Something is frequently overlooked in the concept of forgiveness. Many sincere believers fail to see the benefit of the memories of past forgiven sins.

For example, if I questioned whether or not I had paid last month's electric bill, I would just go through my canceled checks and confirm that it was paid. I have never been depressed over realizing a past bill has already been paid. On the contrary, whenever a past forgiven sin comes back to our minds, we often get depressed, feel discouraged, and even re-confess that same forgiven sin. I wish I had a dollar for every time I heard a counselee say, "Oh, I confessed that sin a year ago—a thousand times." First, that is 999 times too many. Second, each subsequent time that sin is confessed, rather than the confession bringing relief, it only reinforces the false belief that it has not been forgiven. Double, or re-confession, only deepens the false belief that we have not been forgiven.

UNFAIR FIGHTING RULE

It is important to remember that forgiving is not the same as forgetting. Forgiving involves purposing in your heart not to bring up the offense again and not to hold it against the offending party. Just like a merchant would not resubmit a previously paid bill as now due.

Often, in a heated fight, a couple may skirt the real issue that needs to be discussed. Instead, one of them will bring up a past offense and use it as a club over the head of the other party. This is an unfair fighting rule. Every couple has its fights, or disagreements, as some prefer to call them. Every couple has its own fighting rules, whether spoken or unspoken. Even so, it is always an inappropriate fighting rule to bring up an offense that has already been forgiven and use it as a weapon to win an argument, punish, or manipulate the other person. This is not living out the reality of true forgiveness as God designed it. It is tantamount to burying the hatchet but leaving the handle exposed to retrieve for later use. However, as we will clarify in greater detail later, there are natural consequences that forgiveness cannot do away with.

It must also be remembered that forgiveness and trust are two separate issues. A wife may forgive her husband for his infidelity, but that does not mean she is obligated to have an instant trust in him. Forgiveness must be granted; trust has to be earned. Many an erring husband beats himself up emotionally when his wife continues to struggle with feelings about his infidelity. He feels that his wife's struggle is an indication that she has not forgiven him and that she never will. No, forgiving and rebuilding trust are two separate issues that have to be addressed on separate levels. Intellectually, as an act of volitional obedience, a wife may forgive her husband. But on an emotional level it may take time, sometimes even years, to heal her broken heart and to rebuild the trust.

Scores of fractured marriages have been saved when the husband has been able to understand these as two separate levels. I recall telling Ken to remember three things when his wife flares up and reminds him of his past "forgiven" adultery. First, do not remind her that she has forgiven him. She is angry, and emotions are not to be reasoned with. Secondly, don't defend the past or remind her how good you have been since your repentance. That is defensiveness, not listening to understand her. Thirdly, do thank her gently for her gift of forgiveness and for sharing with you just how deeply your adultery hurt her. Most adultery victims are begging for this emotional understanding. Just the sincere acknowledgment of her deep emotional distress could work wonders in facilitating healing in the relationship.

FORGIVEN BUT NOT FORGOTTEN

I could tell by Nancy's facial expression that she was not fully convinced that forgiving is not the same as forgetting. She knew she should forgive but the memories made her feel that she either could not or did not forgive. I asked her, "Is the apostle Paul supposed to be an example to us? Did he not say, 'I exhort you therefore, be imitators of me'" (1 Cor. 4:16)? She nodded in agreement. I then began to explain a truth that is frequently overlooked by many who write and speak on this subject.

PAUL'S HURTS

Paul never forgot what had been done to him. He had been deeply hurt by Alexander, the coppersmith (Acts 19:33). Paul recounted that hurt to Timothy and said, "Alexander the coppersmith did me much harm; the Lord will repay him according to his deeds" (2 Tim. 4:14).

However, note Paul's pattern in dealing with Alexander. First, he remembered what was done to him. Then he recalled what he "did" with what was done to him. He remembered both the offense and what he had done with the offense; namely, he had forgiven Alexander by turning him over to Christ.

I remember when I was a boy and black and white television first came out. One of the most frequent types of programs were Westerns. Every good guy carried two guns, one on each hip. For some reason, the bad guys only carried one gun. When the hero was about to have a shoot-out with the villain, he always drew both guns simultaneously with lightning speed.

Let's suppose for a moment that the gun in the left hand represents the memory of a sin and the gun in the right hand represents the forgiveness of that sin. Each time the gun in the left hand is drawn (memory of a sin), the gun in the right hand should also be drawn (remembering when that sin was forgiven). Better yet, we should tie the two gun barrels together so it would be impossible to pull one gun out without the other. Purpose in your heart that when you remember a past sin, you will also remember the forgiveness you received for that sin.

I have been told by counselees that they were instructed by others not to dwell on past hurts or offenses, but to focus entirely on the future. Each time I am told this I inquire, "Did it work?"

"Well, I guess not" is the candid admission. After establishing the reality of the ineffectiveness of this counsel, I ask, "Do you know why it does not work?" The answer is simple—they were only told half of the process. It is true that we are not to dwell on the past unless we simultaneously focus on what we did with the past from a biblical perspective.

PAUL'S SIN

Paul never forgot his own past sin, even though he knew it was forgiven. While illustrating to Timothy how he, Paul, was an example of God's grace, he recounted that he had formerly been "a blasphemer and a persecutor and a violent aggressor" (1 Tim. 1:13). He even declared to Timothy that Jesus came into the world to save sinners, "among whom I am foremost" (1 Tim. 1:15). Paul uses a present tense verb here, denoting that he is right now the chief of sinners. Question: Was Paul still blaspheming, persecuting, and assaulting fellow Christians? Of course not! In his mind he still remembered what he had done. But he also recalled that he was forgiven and why he received this grace: "And yet for this reason I found mercy, in order that in me as the foremost [sinner], Jesus Christ might demonstrate His perfect patience, as an example for those who would believe in Him for eternal life" (1 Tim. 1:16). Paul successfully integrated his forgiven past into a purposeful memory that became the basis for his present and continued ministry. Paul saw himself as a trophy of grace to be displayed and followed, not an object of shame to be avoided.

King David never forgot his adultery with Bathsheba and the subsequent murder of her husband, Uriah. He was forgiven by God, at least by the time Nathan the prophet confronted him (2 Sam. 12:13). But David wrote later: "For I know my transgressions, and my sin is ever before me" (Ps. 51:3). In the rebuilding process, David knew that he would be able to "teach transgressors Thy ways, and [as a result] sinners will be converted to Thee" (Ps. 51:13).

Nevertheless, if Paul had followed the popular counsel to forget the sins that had been forgiven, we would have been robbed of one of the most profound declarations of grace. We see the hallmark of this assertion couched in an open admission of Paul's personal unworthiness to be an apostle: "For I am the least of the apostles who am not fit to be called an apostle," Why? "Because I persecuted the church of God." Then reality sets in, "But by the grace of God I am what I am" (2 Cor. 15:9–11).

Paul's appreciation for the grace of God was in direct proportion to the memories of his forgiven past. This explains why those who are of the forgive-and-forget persuasion usually have less appreciation for grace and a greater emphasis on legalistic works which result in pride. They latently feel they have earned their "godly" standing. Jesus made this point clear in the parable of the pharisee and the tax collector which He told to those who trusted in their own righteousness and viewed others with contempt (Luke 18:9–14).

Paul's past memories not only put his apostleship in perspective, but also his standing as a saint. He felt he was the very least of all of the saints, but through grace he was able to preach to the Gentiles the unfathomable riches of Christ (Eph. 3:8).

"Fine," you say, "but he did not remind others of their past sins." Not so. When he told the Corinthian church who would not inherit the kingdom of God, he spelled out their former sins: ". . .fornicators, idolaters, adulterers, homosexuals, thieves, covetous, drunkards . . . ." Then, to reduce any holier-than-thou attitudes among his readers, he reminded them, "and such were some of you." But don't stop there. Read on: "But you were washed . . . sanctified . . . justified in the name of the Lord Jesus Christ" (2 Cor. 6:9–11).

Again, note the pattern: He recalled their sin, but he also recalled what they had done with their sin. It was forgiven, but not forgotten. Yet it was recalled in the context of how it had been dealt with. The memories were to serve as a reminder of the process of forgiveness—forgiveness not just of past offenses, but of any future ones as well.

JOSEPH NEVER FORGOT

Jacob's son Joseph is often used as an Old Testament type of Christ. Yet he also serves as a classic example of one who had to forgive a major personal hurt, but who never forgot it happened.

Joseph had been kidnapped, sold to Ishmaelite traders, and wound up as a slave in Egypt (Gen. 37:28,36). Later there was a reconciliation with his brothers (Gen. 45:5–8), but the brothers assumed that Joseph had not taken revenge on them only because their father was still alive. When their father died, panic set in. The brothers approached Joseph to ask that he spare their lives (Gen. 50:15–17).

In response, Joseph made two profound statements: "You

meant evil against me [their sin], but God meant it for good . . . to preserve many people alive" [God's purpose] (Gen. 50:20). Joseph never forgot the evil perpetrated against him by his brothers, but he forgave them, and then viewed their sin against him from God's perspective. He never excused their sin, but he forgave it and put a new meaning on it which he, too, had to learn from God.

"Yes," Nancy interrupted, "but I remember my dad using Joseph as an example of how God made him forget all his troubles and all his father's household" (Gen. 41:51). Nancy had unintentionally just given another hint of why it is hard for some people to forgive. I reminded Nancy of something she was very familiar with, namely, the importance of using Scripture to interpret Scripture. In the very same chapter that Joseph names his first born son Manasseh (which means "making to forget"), it was recorded that Joseph began a very vigorous and demanding undertaking.

At the age of thirty, Joseph began his service under Pharaoh. He commenced a seven-year food conservation program by extensively surveying the land (v. 46). For seven years he personally supervised the gathering of all the food which was to be stored in preparation for the predicted famine. Storage had to be located in each city near the fields (v. 48). The quantity of the grain was in such abundance that they stopped measuring it, for it was beyond measure (v. 49).

It was in the sixth year of this very demanding project that Manasseh was born to Asenath, Joseph's wife. By naming him Manasseh, Joseph was attempting to remind himself that he had forgotten all of his family troubles (v. 51). Although he credits God for making him *forget* all his family losses, the reality of it was, God kept him so busy he did not have time to remember or recall the pain of the losses.

When Joseph viewed his brothers for the first time in fourteen years, Scripture says, " . . . and Joseph remembered the dreams which he had about them" (Gen. 42:9). Furthermore, three days later, when Joseph overheard his brothers acknowledge that all their troubles were because they sold him into slavery, Joseph turned away from them and wept. Why? He apparently had buried the emotional hurt for so long, that it now erupted to the surface.

Had Joseph indeed forgotten his brothers' offenses? No. Was he over the emotional pain? Apparently not. But the crucial point is that he was able to refocus because God kept him purposefully busy.

Busyness is a drug of choice for many hurting people. Many fill their lives with activities to prevent feelings of past hurts from coming into their minds. Like them, Joseph was able to deny, stuff, suppress, or ignore past hurts through excessive activity. The harder one works at staying busy to avoid painful memories and the resulting emotions, the harder it is to forgive as time passes. Time does not heal wounds as many profess. It only postpones the process of healing. No one has ever told me that it is easier to forgive today than it was years ago when a particular devastating event happened. In fact, I have discovered for myself that it is actually much harder.

I personally believe that God's timing for us always comes before we think we are ready. He gives us less than twelve hours—before sunset. But for many, days stretch into years, and they find themselves in the sunset of their lives before they make peace with the past through the godly gift of forgiveness. Unfortunately, the longer it takes, the harder it gets—and the more likely it becomes that forgiveness may never happen.

Joseph never completely forgot what his brothers did. The press of the pending famine and mammoth food storage program only kept his mind off of it. But in time he ultimately had to face it. When he did, his entire family became reconciled through forgiveness and through viewing God's purpose for the hurtful acts in the first place.

At this point, it was evident to Nancy that Scripture was clear on the forgive-and-forget issue. But one lingering doubt remained in her mind: "Paul and Joseph forgave and still remembered, but all those problem verses I had quoted were about people, not God." Where in the Bible does it ever say that God forgives yet still remembers?

JESUS AND THE HARLOT

I turned in my Bible to Luke chapter seven and asked her to read the story of Jesus and the harlot. Nancy reviewed the story of how this forgiven prostitute had slipped into Simon's dinner party and knelt down at Jesus' feet, washing them with her tears of gratefulness and wiping them with her hair. Then I asked Nancy pointedly if Jesus was God at the time He was upon the earth. She instantly responded with a theologically correct affirmative. Then I zeroed in on verse 47. Jesus, looking at the harlot but addressing his host Simon, the Pharisee, said, "For this reason I say to you, her sins, which are many, have been forgiven." It is interesting to note here that the Greek verb translated "have been forgiven" is in the perfect tense. This means that the action (the forgiveness) happened in the past but has results that continue up to the present and will continue into the future. Apparently sometime in the near past, Jesus had met her and forgiven her for her immorality. He not only said "her sins," but He added, "which are many." He knew the full extent of her sordid past.

"Now," I challenged Nancy again, "was Jesus God?"

"Yes."

"Did He forgive her?"

"Yes."

"Did He forget what she had done?"

"No."

Here is God in the flesh, forgiving sins, yet still remembering them. He did not have amnesia and wonder why this woman was washing His feet with her tears and wiping them with her hair. He remembered the extent of the sin for which she had been forgiven! In fact He will never forget, even in eternity, what she or we did to Him. He is referred to as "the Lamb" over twenty-five times in the book of Revelation. What kind of Lamb? A slain Lamb (Rev. 5:6–8). Why was He slain? The apostle John explains, "For thou wast slain, and didst purchase for God with Thy blood men from every tribe and tongue and people and nation" (Rev. 5:9). The Lord Jesus Christ is going to live out eternity—not forgetting what he has forgiven—but forgiving and being praised by those who have been forgiven. And we are going to join the heavenly throng and say with a loud voice, "Worthy is the Lamb that was slain to receive power and riches and wisdom and might and honor and glory and blessing" (Rev. 5:12). Why? Because we will never forget the debt He paid for us. Praise God!

But Jesus seized the opportunity with Simon and the forgiven harlot to give one of the most important reasons we should never forget what we have been forgiven. He gently declared that she was doing this because she "loved much." Her forgiven past was the basis for her present and deep love for the Lord. Why? Because "he who is forgiven little, loves little" (Luke 7:47). Or to put it another way, he who remembers being forgiven much, loves much. This understanding of how our Lord forgives but does not forget became the key to Laura's freedom.

LIBERATED MOM

The fourth session of the Single Parents' Retreat had concluded. Each mom or dad made their way to the scenic amphitheater overlooking the large spring-fed lake. The 104° North Platte, Nebraska, prairie had cooled down to a "comfortable" 89° that evening. It was a praise and sharing time.

Before the camp staff brought the children to the amphitheater to join their parents, Laura took this opportunity to share her newfound inner freedom. Many parents had already conveyed their gratefulness for the outstanding facilities, food, graded children's program, and messages. As we all stood up for a stretch break, Laura walked up to me and said, "I want to thank you for something you said today. You can't believe the relief I feel." The tears began to trickle down her cheeks. "For years I believed a lie that totally controlled my thoughts about God and myself."

Laura recalled some advice she had received from a sincere youth pastor years ago: "forgive and forget." His well-intended advice was supposed to be the key to peace with her past hurts and the cure for any discomfort from her pain. Unfortunately, her humanity got in the way. At any given moment her past would flash into the present and haunt her. Laura logically concluded two things: first, she must not have truly been forgiven because these memories still nagged her, and second, that's why she could not be forgiven. This second distortion thwarted her concept of God. She reasoned, "Every time I remember my past sin, it must be because God has not forgiven me, otherwise, why can't I forget it?" Laura's memories screamed at her, "You haven't been forgiven, and God has not forgiven you either."

Then Laura shared what had liberated her. "Today, Chuck, when you said that God does not forget our sin and that our brain was designed not to forget, it sounded too good to be true. But you're right. An omniscient God does not forget, but He chooses not to hold forgiven sins against us. Then, when you said that our remaining memories were designed to be a source of praise, thanksgiving, and gratefulness (Luke 7:47), that really made sense."

By now the children began to arrive. Laura glanced at the excited kids, and then back to me. "I hope I can convey this to my kids." And I believe she will. An imprisoned mom has become a liberated mom. For the truth of God's Word has set her free (John 8:31–32).

For me, the forgive-and-forget theology helps explain the ever-present coldness of those who, like Simon, are theologically straight as an arrow, orthodox to the hilt, but relationally very cold. They may have gained much in the way of biblical knowledge, but they have forgotten what they have been forgiven. I do not say this to be critical. It is only a natural result of the forgive-and-forget thinking.

I believe memories of past forgiveness were the motivation for Isaac Watts who penned these words to his famous hymn:

> *Oh to grace how great a debtor*
> *daily I'm constrained to be.*
> *Let Thy mercies like a fetter*

bind my wandering heart to Thee.
Prone to wander, Lord, I feel it,
prone to leave the God I love.
Take my heart, oh, take and seal it,
seal it to Thy courts above.

MEMORY FLASHBACKS

"I guess it's not that I haven't forgiven my dad, it's that I don't know what to do with the memories." Nancy had just taken one of the most significant steps leading to inner healing—she recognized the distinction between forgiving and forgetting.

Remember, forgiving and forgetting are two separate issues. The process of working through forgiveness and dealing with memories is really a two-pronged process. If the two are not separated, forgiveness will be much harder.

What do you do with the memories? First, we will look at the memories of our own offenses. Then, we will look at what we can do with the painful memories of others' offenses against us.

OUR SINFUL MEMORIES

I recall driving down an interstate with the cruise control on, and casually enjoying the scenery. All of the sudden, a memory of a past forgiven sin I had committed sprang into my mind. Just as quickly as the memory appeared, so did the emotion of guilt and especially shame. In a split second I went from praise to the pits.

Our emotions usually play off of our thoughts. You think sad thoughts and you will feel sad. Have you ever heard someone say, "The more I think about it the madder I get?" This is the reason I will ask a counselee to tell me about his feelings—they give me a clue as to what his thoughts are.

I asked myself why I felt depressed when I remembered my forgiven sin. It was obvious. I was still feeling guilt and shame for this forgiven sin. Then I asked myself, "Am I worthy of guilt and shame for this sin?" The answer is no. It has been confessed and forgiven.

As the intruding memory sprang to my mind, I did three things:

1) *I Addressed God.* I said, emphatically, out loud: "God!" That stopped the intrusive thought temporarily because it factored God back into the process.

2) *I Thanked God.* As an act of my will I said: "Thank You, God, for allowing this memory to come to my mind, and thank You for already forgiving me and affirming that I am no longer worthy of blame and shame."

3) *I Praised God.* It was only then that I could break forth in a song of praise, expressing my love to Him.

What started out as a trip to the pits of despair ended in the heights of praise—all from the same memory. My recall became an opportunity to praise God for His forgiveness. It did not drive me to re-confession and deeper doubt and despair, but to praise. It is one thing to recall a sin, but it's an entirely different thing to relive it—especially apart from forgiveness.

My car is equipped with two visual sources. One is a windshield and another a rear vision mirror. The mirror represents my past. I can glance at it from time to time, but I cannot change what I have driven by. The windshield is my present and distant future. I can still make corrections in the present to reduce potential conflicts in the future. If I reverse the functions, I could experience a serious wreck. If I drive forward, but constantly stare into the rear vision mirror, the obvious will happen. But if I focus through the windshield, and only glance in the rear vision mirror, I will stay on track and arrive safely.

"Yes, but what if that recalled memory was placed there by Satan?" you may ask (Rev. 12:10). "Or what if God's Spirit brought it up to my mind?" (Not likely. God's Spirit does not accuse the saint for confessed sin—see Rom. 8:33.) "Or what if it just came out of my memory bank?" The answer is simple. It makes no difference where the memory came from. Just process it in the same way, and it will end up in praise to God.

SINS AGAINST US

When we recall our past offenses, we tend to respond with guilt or shame. When we recall others' sins against us, we usually respond in renewed anger. If we learn to remember the principle of the "sin memory" gun and the "forgiveness memory" gun each time we recall an offense, we will also recall what we did with that offense. At first we may have to force ourselves to make this double recall, but as we do our response will be similar to what I did with my own sin:

Address God. Stating God's name in a firm way forcibly stops the obsessive thinking, but usually only momentarily. It is like the first gear in a three-speed transmission. The first gear is only designed to get you started; it is not the one you continue to drive in.

Thank God. Express appreciation to God for allowing you to remember the past offense you had to forgive. It allows you to review this biblical tool which Christ illustrated at the time of His own hurt and rejection (Luke 23:34). Also, it will bring to mind what you did to the offender by placing him in the "Jesus jail," a concept we will discuss in the next chapter. You can thank Him that you were able to give the same gift of forgiveness you received and thus reflect God's character to others.

Praise God. Sincerely praise God for the tool of forgiveness. Praise Him for forgiving you as you forgive others (Matt. 6:12) and for what He is going to do through this experience for His glory. What is the net result of both memories? PRAISE!

NO ROOM

Reflecting on the source of the forgive-and-forget perspective, it finally dawned on me one reason it has developed. Before we forgive someone, the constant pain from their hurt can be all consuming—a "10" on a scale of 1 to 10. After forgiving them that pain may reduce to a "2" or even a "1." Because forgiveness can be such an emotional release and relief, we feel much better, and the intensity of the memory is greatly or even entirely reduced. With this great reduction of the pain, the memory of it also fades. This memory fade is commonly assumed to be part and parcel of forgiveness. Forgiving and forgetting is an experience common to many and is assumed to be mutually inclusive. But is not true for all. The memories may fade or they may not. But the presence of the memory is not a factor in forgiveness. May it be true of us all what was said of Abraham Lincoln: "His heart had no room for the memory of a wrong."

FORGETTING THE PAST

Because memory fade is so closely associated with forgiveness, a proof text for the forgive-and-forget experience is sought. If it is "true," it must be in the Bible. Yes, a proof text is available. Sally reminded me of it. "Didn't the apostle Paul say, 'But this one thing I do, forgetting those things which are behind, and reaching forth unto those things which are before' (Phil. 3:13 KJV)? If he could do it, I should be able to do it."

Proof texts are often just like that—isolated verses taken out of context to prove one's experience. How do you explain Philippians 3:13 to Sally? Simple. In verses one through sixteen, Paul is simply explaining that all of his religious and academic accomplishments and status among men are now regarded by him as rubbish compared to knowing the Lord Jesus Christ and all he gained in Him (Phil. 3:8). He is not forgetting his past sins, he is forgetting his status, acclaim, accomplishments, and prestige; and focusing on (reaching toward) the goal which lies ahead of him.

MOTIVATION TO SERVE

There is a great debate over what is the highest motivation to serve God. May I suggest one of the best, if not the best? Love for Christ. Paul stated this in Second Corinthians 5:14: "For the love of Christ controls us . . .." Paul's sacrificial service was not based on guilt for the gross sins he had committed prior to his conversion. No, it sprang from his love for Christ because of the forgiveness he received. Paul did not try to repay God for his past sin. Rather, he lived out a life of love and appreciation for the forgiveness Christ had already granted.

There is a world of difference between serving God to get Him to do something for you, or to repay Him for something, and serving Him out of appreciation for what He has already done (Rom. 12:1). Paul did not perform for God to get His acceptance. Instead, he served because he had already been accepted in Christ and he wanted to express his love and appreciation for that reality.

RELIEF

Nancy began to relax. The burden of the false belief she had carried for so many years was lifted from her shoulders. She was able to distinguish between forgiveness and memories. A quiet confidence replaced her anxiety as she realized what she would do when the memories returned. It was no longer hard to forgive her dad.

◊

Unlike Nancy, Fred was not even at first base with forgiveness. He felt his dad should pay for the pain he had inflicted on him. Fred was right. Someone should pay for that pain.

Chapter 4

"Someone Has to Pay!"

F*red knows the Bible*. In fact, there is not a theological issue that he has not studied thoroughly for himself. His personal library could be the envy of any aspiring pastor. His commitment to Jesus Christ as Lord and Savior was firm, and his church involvement as an adult was impressive.

"I know I shouldn't feel this way," Fred began, "but I can't help it. I just don't think God loves me." The look of despair on his face confirmed the desperation in his voice.

"Why do Christians have these feelings? Doesn't becoming a Christian change all that junk? I guess it just doesn't work for dumb, fat, ugly people like me," he concluded, as his eyes dropped to the floor.

After a little prodding, Fred began to share the heartrending story of an alcoholic father who did not want him and an angry mother who lashed out in rage and destructive criticism. It became evident that Fred had some unfinished business with both parents, but especially with his father.

Fred's father treated him like a rejected little brother, not like a son. He could never lose a game, especially to Fred. He favored Fred's younger sister and was openly cruel to

Fred. He came from a background of alcohol and abuse, and he reproduced this "heritage" in his own adulthood.

CAN'T FORGIVE

After Fred reeled off a whole list of deep hurts of rejection, isolation, abandonment, favoritism, and ridicule, I gently broached the subject of Fred's response to his father's offenses: "Your father has deeply hurt you."

"Yeah, but I haven't told you the half of it. I guess you've got the idea. Besides, I don't like talking about it." Fred's reasoning was logical. "If I don't talk about it, I don't have to think about it. If I don't have to think about it, I won't have to feel it." It is the potential of re-experiencing past hurtful emotions that makes the goal of forgiveness very hard. But the offenses have to be identified before they can be forgiven.

To Fred's assertion, I countered: "A past that is not processed is always present in one form or another." Problems that are not worked out will be acted out, and that acting out is often more painful than working through the issue, both for the one doing it and for those around him.

"What are you doing with all that deep hurt and pain?" I asked.

"Stuffing it."

"Has that been effective in your overall spiritual or mental health?"

"It's worked so far."

"Is that why you are in my office today?"

"Yes, well . . . no. I mean . . . I guess it has worked for awhile, but now the abuse will not leave my mind. I've got to get rid of this stuff. I mean, it happened so long ago, and my dad is dead. I need to get a life!"

"What choices do you have about your memories of your dad?"

"I know where you're heading with that question, so I might as well make it clear to you up front: I know I should forgive my dad but I can't—ever! I've tried, and it doesn't work. I just can't let him off the hook that easily after all he's done to me."

"SCOT-FREE"

Fred believed another false idea that makes it hard to forgive. He sincerely believed that, if he forgave his dad, his dad would be off "scot-free." That is, he would go unpunished. The logic of this idea implies that payment or revenge must precede forgiveness. What Fred did not understand is that he was absolutely right. Someone must pay for the deep crushing hurts he received. Even the Bible underscores this need: " . . . without shedding of blood there is no forgiveness . . ." (Heb. 9:22).

In the written record and/or oral tradition of most every culture, there are revenge laws. Personally, I believe the need to get revenge is in the heart of every man from birth. Cain killed Abel out of jealous revenge. God accepted Abel's offering, but not Cain's. God even told him what he could do to correct it. Cain refused and killed his brother instead (Gen. 4:1–8).

The principle of satisfying justice by taking revenge may be a part of the general revelation to all men (Rom. 1:19). It was even the basis for the Mosaic law, an "eye for an eye" (Exod. 21:24). We see it, too, in the earliest recorded law in the world, the Code of Hammurabi. This written code dates back to ancient Babylon and is almost four thousand years old.

Human logic says that my offender is deserving of punishment, and I must exact that punishment or see to it that it is exacted before I forgive. There are at least two small problems with that conviction. First, it is true that offenders deserve—and need—to be punished. But we must hand over the responsibility of carrying out the punishment to someone else, if for no other reason than that it takes a righteous judge to exact true justice. No one is one hundred percent objective and impartial. Peter clarifies that God is the only one who judges righteously and impartially (1 Pet. 2:23). Secondly, very few offenses can be adequately "paid for," and seldom does the offended party have the power or opportunity to exact the payment. When repayment is not possible, revenge becomes the next best thing.

However, without the universal law that someone must pay for offenses and not just let people off the hook and go scot-free, the death of Christ on the cross does not make sense. You cannot separate justice and revenge. Without the cross, there would be no moral basis for forgiveness. Why? Because someone has to pay. Fred's right!

Fred falsely reasoned that if he withheld forgiveness from his dad, he was in some small way exacting revenge on his father. Fred believed that his bitterness would somehow hurt his deceased father and give relief to himself. The problem with that reasoning is at least threefold: 1) it does not work, 2) it is not right, and 3) it destroys or punishes the wrong person, i.e., Fred. He was bludgeoning himself emotionally and also, unknowingly his family.

This is why the writer of Hebrews issues such a strong

warning, "See to it that no one comes short of the grace of God; that no root of bitterness springing up causes trouble, and by it many be defiled" (Heb. 12:15).

Bitterness is like a rock thrown into a placid pond; after its initial splash, it sends out concentric circles that disturb the whole pond. It starts with ourselves, expands to our spouse, then to our children, friends, and colleagues.

Peter saw this beginning in Simon who tried to buy the Holy Spirit: "For I see that you are in the gall of bitterness and in the bondage of iniquity" (Acts 8:23). The word *gall* refers to a sore spot resulting from repeated rubbing. The mental "rubbing" or ruminating over past offenses only deepens the wound and destroys one's peace.

BUT WHO'S GOING TO PAY?

There is usually a difference between how men and women view revenge. Women usually do not want to inflict physical pain on the offender. Rather, their desire is that the offender understand, or feel, how they have hurt them. Women tend to express their anger verbally. Men tend to experience the need to punish physically. Fred was no exception.

I could see from Fred's agitation that our discussion of forgiveness was not setting well with him. Out of my peripheral vision I saw my oak desk, and an idea struck me.

"Fred, what would your father have to experience before you would be willing to release him?"

He shrugged his shoulders indifferently.

Then I asked him, "What if your father were here in this office and I had him take his shirt off and lay across my desk. Then I took a cat-o'-nine-tails [a whip with leather thongs and jagged metal pieces tied to the ends] and began to whip your father across his back. If I whipped him five times would you be able to release him?"

"No!"

"What if I struck him ten times?"

Fred's stern look said, "No."

Then I encouraged Fred to visualize graphically his father receiving thirty-nine lashes (see Matt. 27:26). And, for emphasis, I suggested smashing his face to the point of non-recognition (see Matt. 26:67; 27:30), and insulting him with verbal curses (see Luke 22:64–65; 23:35–37; Matt. 27:39).

Fred crossed his arms with an "I-know-what-you're-doing" look on his face. But I didn't stop. As I described dragging thorny branches across his head (John 19:2), Fred rolled his eyes in disgust. I spoke of spitting in his face (Matt. 26:67), embarrassing or shaming him in front of his friends and family (John 19:25–26), driving spikes into his hands and feet (John 20:27), and isolating him from his friends (Matt. 27:27).

An amazing thing happened. Fred's countenance began to soften. God's Spirit hit His mark. Why such a graphic depiction of the death of Christ? What is the purpose? Simple: to remind us of three major truths we often forget. The first one is that someone has to pay for our pain and offenses and that someone was Christ. The spirit of revenge in every culture in our world today underscores that. This truth is obvious. The second major truth is just as obvious, yet it is often forgotten and unrecognized because along with its admission comes an implicit responsibility—the responsibility to forgive. That truth is that Jesus died for the sins of our offenders as well as for our own! When asked, "Why did Jesus die on the cross?" Christians usually parrot the expected response: "For our sin." When we probe deeper, "Who else's sin did

Jesus die for?" the unforgiving person's response is slower. To admit we know Christ died for the sin of the offender as well as our own is hard to acknowledge. Why? Because we may still feel the offender has to pay a price for their sin against us.

The third truth we are reminded of by Christ's brutal death is that the cross explains how hard it was for God Himself to forgive. The price required to pay for our sins was extremely high, and only God could pay such a high price.

DOUBLE PAYMENT

Recall my experience with the large gas bill. The clerk did not feel it was fair that the manager chose to pay for my mistake. The question in her mind was not whether the bill was paid, but who should pay it. Her reasoning was clear: If I incur the bill, I should pay. Here again we are confronted with the innate sense of fairness and revenge. The one who commits the offense must pay, not someone else. This is not fair or right.

This reasoning creates two problems. First, it implies that every bill incurred by a person can easily be paid. Consider, for example, a careless camper who fails to extinguish his campfire. The fire is later fanned into a massive forest fire, which destroys millions of dollars of property in the process. He wouldn't have the ability to repay his debt, even if he lived a hundred lifetimes! No, not every offense can be repaid. Where restitution is possible, it is right for the restitution to be made. But the fact remains that there is no way humanly possible to repay most of us for the deep hurts we've had to bear. There is nothing my father could do to repay me for the emotional pain he inflicted. This is the reason forgiveness is never a receipt for payment in full. It is a pardon that is totally undeserved (Eph. 2:8–9).

Even God affirms this. The writer of Hebrews sets the record straight: "For it is impossible for the blood of bulls and goats to take away sins" (Heb. 10:4). Yes, but what about all the massive sacrifices in the Old Testament? Didn't they pay for the people's sin? The answer is, no. Those sacrifices only covered the sin temporarily, until the ultimate sacrifice, the Lamb of God, came to pay for all sin—past, present, future (John 1:29). In reality, no one can inflict the depth of pain and revenge that an offender deserves.

Second, the clerk's insistence that I pay the bill as well is ludicrous. Double payment is not justice. Even our country's judicial system underscores this with its concept of "double jeopardy." According to the laws of our land, a person cannot be tried for the same crime twice. Failing to forgive a person because they themselves have not paid for the offense is implying that Jesus Christ and the offender must pay. Is double payment ultimately just?

Scripture makes it quite clear that Jesus died for the sins of the whole world (John 3:16)—including the sins of our offenders! What God did was to take the offender's sin, and place the penalty (i.e., payment) on Jesus: "He [God] made Him [Jesus] who knew no sin to be sin on our behalf, that we might become the righteousness of God in Him" (2 Cor. 5:21). God paid a debt He did not owe for man who owed a debt to God that he could not pay. Honestly, Jesus paid the cost of forgiveness (1 Pet. 2:24). This is the reason it takes a partnership of two to work through to forgiveness—God and you.

Most, if not all, offenders are unable to repay the depth of pain they have caused. And even if they could, it would be tantamount to double jeopardy. If they could, they would have to meet God's criteria before their sacrifice would actually pay for their offenses: they would have to be perfect. Obviously, all offenders fail on that count.

God's Spirit was dealing with Fred. He knew intellectually that Christ had died not only for his sins, but also for those of his father. But there was something Fred still had to do with his father's offenses against him because it was still too hard to forgive.

MAJOR TRANSFER

At this point it was important to reiterate to Fred just whose responsibility it is to exact revenge. According to God's Word, God's justice may include revenge. But the question is, "Who is divinely ordained to do it?" Paul clarified this matter with the Roman Christians when he said, "Never take your own revenge, beloved, but leave room for the wrath of God, for it is written, 'Vengeance is Mine, I will repay,' says the Lord" (Rom. 12:19).

God declares that He is the Divine Bill Collector. He merely asks us to "leave room," or "get out of the way," so that He can deal with the person directly. He illustrated this with Lot at the destruction of Sodom and Gomorrah (Gen. 19). God had judged these twin cities because of their decadent immorality. But He would not rain down judgment until righteous Lot and his family had vacated the cities cited for doom.

Quite often an offender cannot hear from God because we are "shouting" in their ears with our feeble attempts at revenge.

So they spend their energy reacting to us and, in the process, ignoring God. But God is the ultimate avenger (1 Thess. 4:6).

When Paul had been hurt by Alexander the coppersmith, he did not forget the offense. But he did remember what he did with the offender—he transferred him to God for payment: "The Lord will repay him according to his deeds" (2 Tim. 4:14b). What is usually overlooked at this point is that Paul had to do a hard thing: he had to trust God. When Paul transferred Alexander over to God, Paul had to trust God to deal with him.

But when one is angry over a deep hurt, trust is one of the first things to go. For example, those who come from a dysfunctional home or malfunctioning environment struggle with at least three issues:

1) *They can't feel.* They do not allow themselves to have feelings, especially anger.

2) *They can't share.* They feel that they would be disloyal or bad (i.e., they would feel shame) if they shared their feelings or offenses with others, even those who could help them.

3) *They can't trust.* They cannot trust anyone outside themselves to protect them or act on their behalf. And that is why it is hard to forgive.

Everyone is dysfunctional to some degree. The only difference is in degree. The Scripture makes it clear that we "all have sinned and fall short" (Rom. 3:23) individually and in our relationships. Therefore, the ability to trust God, especially in the area of revenge, is a challenge even for the best of us; thus it is hard to forgive.

Now that we understand the difficulty of trusting God to deal with the offender, how can we trustingly transfer an offender over to God? The first step is to examine our motivation for doing so. Basically, there are three levels of motivation. The highest, of course, is doing something for God just because God said so. It takes a great deal of maturity to do this. Next is the level of doing something for the sake of others. This has a greater appeal for most. However, if one is in the grip of bitterness, the "I-don't-care-what-others-think" feeling quickly eliminates that. The third level of motivation is basically a concern for my own personal gain or loss. This was the level where Fred was stuck. I knew I had to have Fred visualize what transference meant, and it had to be at his level of motivation. I drew this word picture in order to portray that concept:

"Fred," I began, "let's suppose you were the sheriff of a small one-horse town in the wild west." (I could see he was with me—he loved John Wayne movies.) I went on to describe a sheriff who had a small cubical for an office and an even smaller holding cell. I encouraged him to visualize that he had just caught a criminal, and that the circuit-riding judge had tried and convicted him. Now the criminal must serve his time in Sheriff Fred's cramped jail cell. Fred has no deputies, so he is totally responsible for the convicted criminal's food, recreation, personal hygiene, and security needs. Fred can't go anywhere. He has to check the jail every few hours. If he goes anywhere for any extended period of time, he has to slap on handcuffs and take the prisoner with him. It wouldn't be such a bother if the sentence was a brief two weeks. But what if it was a life sentence?

Let's suppose that Sheriff Fred gets a letter from the county seat stating that they have just completed the construction of a three-story jail, with twenty-four-hour guard service and total care provided. The only requirement is that you have to bring the prisoner down personally and provide a copy of all the trial and conviction papers.

"Fred," I began slowly, "you have a choice. You can either keep your father imprisoned in your heart and be totally responsible for him, or you can transfer him to the county seat and let him serve out his sentence there."

This may be the hardest choice a person has to make in life. He can either continue to keep the offender imprisoned in his heart and suffer in bitterness or turn over to Jesus the person who rightfully deserves to suffer.

He was quiet. He knew his dad was in jail either way—he was in his jail or in the "Jesus jail."

Fred knew down deep he should forgive, but it was hard to let go. His whole life had revolved around bitterness toward his dad and it was not easy to release him. But Fred's countenance brightened. I could see he had decided what to do.

It was amazing. Just an hour before, he was not willing to forgive his dad. Now he was eager to. Why? Because he had struggled with a core belief that to forgive meant to forego punishment. The offender would be off scot-free. There would be no punishment or revenge. That is unfair. But when he grasped the concept that someone did pay, that revenge is biblical (if God does it), that double payment is not justice, and that his heart does not have to be a prison any longer, he was free. Free to bury his last symbol of revenge, his hatchet of bitterness.

It was time to make a major transfer. I asked Fred to pray with me. I led him in a phrase-by-phrase prayer. I asked him to picture putting his dad in a car, driving to the county jail, and pulling up to the receiving area, only to be greeted by someone in a white robe, beard, sandals, and nail-scarred hands. I asked him to walk his dad up to Jesus, and then I paused. At this point I told Fred to tell Jesus, in his own words, how his dad had hurt him, and that he was now turning him over to Him.

The tears flowed. The hidden pain of years past now surfaced. But we were not yet finished. I instructed him to tell the Lord that He was free to exact revenge or punishment on his father. That was the easy part. Then I had Fred ask the Lord to grant his father grace (Eph. 2:8–9); mercy (Rom. 12:1); pardon (Matt. 6:12); and even bless him if He chose (Luke 6:28), just as he had done for Fred.

Forgiveness brought a flood of release and freedom from bitterness. A new insight hit Fred. All these years he had thought his dad was the prisoner and he, Fred, was the warden. He realized that day that he had been the prisoner of his own bitterness.

As a boy I remember seeing an old movie on the life of two prison guards. The last scene from that film has stayed with me all of these years. As the two guards stood at their post watching a longtime prisoner finally being released after years of incarceration, one guard turned to the other and said: "These guys come and go, but we stay. I wonder who the real prisoners are?" The result of forgiveness is setting the prisoner free, and finally realizing you yourself were the prisoner.

I MUST PAY

Fred felt his dad must pay. But Darren, another "prisoner," felt he himself must pay. Darren was a major substance abuser.

If it was addictive, he used it. But his addictive behavior went beyond the pleasure-seeking or mind-numbing cycle. He was bent on self-destruction. I wish I could say I helped him and he is now living a very meaningful and productive life. Regretfully, this is not the case.

Just as people turn anger on themselves, they also turn punishment on themselves. His logic could not be penetrated. He said he knew he should be forgiven but he just could not forgive himself for the atrocities he committed in Vietnam. However, his core issue was his refusal to see and accept God's forgiveness. He obsessively focused on the perceived evil of his own heart and sought to punish himself for his past. Pain felt good because pain was consistent with what he believed he deserved. And apart from the substitutionary, sacrificial death of Christ on that Roman cross, he is right.

But self-inflicted pain is often rooted in the lie, "I must pay for my sin." This is a major deception. If Darren was to live a hundred lifetimes of self-inflicted pain, he could never repay or make up for his sin. The good news is that it has already been paid for and that Darren has only to receive the pardon, just as a pardon is granted by a governor. But if Darren refuses to accept the pardon, the penalty remains. If it remains, the deception leads us to believe that we now deserve to destroy ourselves because of false repayment (i.e., trying to pay sin's penalty ourselves). Again, Darren's loss came by the blindness of his own understanding of God's forgiveness, not the perceived need to forgive himself.

Some people are more subtle than Darren with their self-destruction. They may choose to take their own life slowly through heavy drinking, smoking, destructive relationships, and even overwork. Many work themselves to death, not in order to provide for their basic needs, but to punish themselves for unprocessed guilt and shame. Why? For them it is too hard to be forgiven. This is one of the reasons God chose Saul to be saved. After all, Saul was a blasphemer, a persecutor, and a violent aggressor toward Christians (1 Tim. 1:13). Then Saul (whose name after conversion is Paul) explained why he was chosen by God: "And yet for this reason I found mercy, in order that in me as the foremost, Jesus Christ might demonstrate His perfect patience, as an example, for those who would believe in Him for eternal life" (1 Tim. 1:16). The logic is simple: If God could forgive Saul (Paul), He could forgive anyone. Everyone else was "down hill" for God.

But Darren refused to see that what Christ did in His death was greater than anything that Darren did in his life. Why couldn't he see it? I know of at least two reasons. First, as a result of unbelief, God does to them what He did to the Jews in Isaiah's day: "He [God] has blinded their eyes, and He has hardened their heart, lest they see with their eyes, and perceive with their heart, and be converted, and I heal them" (John 12:40). Secondly, the Apostle Paul explains why the gospel is veiled from the unbelieving: because "the god of this world [Satan] has blinded the minds of the unbelieving, that they might not see the light of the gospel of the glory of Christ, who is the image of God" (2 Cor. 4:3-4). Satan takes the words of hope and release sown in the heart and snatches them away, greatly increasing the difficulty to forgive (Luke 8:12).

Fortunately, this was not so with Fred. He was able to see that Christ's horrific death more than paid for his dad's sin. It was enough for him. It was enough for Pam, too.

GOD IN THE LOBBY

Most counseling at Living Foundation Ministries takes place in one of the staff offices. Pam, however, did business with God in the lobby. As a staff member was meeting with her teenage son, she thought she would catch up on some reading. Her eyes fell upon a draft manuscript copy of *Bury the Hatchet*. Her stomach tightened. Not this again. I'm going to let her tell you her story:

The bookcase was full of other options. I was drawn by the powder blue cover. But God drew me to the title. I thumbed it. Before I knew it, I was reading it. I wasn't pre-pared for what happened. My mid-life mind drifted back to a shy "love needy" 15-year-old girl.

I was flirty. I pursued attention and affection. My pas-tor was vulnerable in his own marriage, I learned years later. He showed me attention and special interest. It was not long before his immoral advances began.

I felt trapped and terribly confused. I would hear one thing from the pulpit and another when I was alone with a man who emotionally and subtly forced his affections on me.

I blamed myself. There had to be something terribly wrong with me to cause a pastor to be immoral. We jointly deceived my family, his family, and the church.

Finally, it all came to light. Endless "what-do-we-do-now meetings" seemed to come and go. So did the years, but not my anger, bitterness, hurt, and emotional pain.

Eventually, I married and had children of my own. I knew I should forgive my pastor but my unwillingness to forgive only embroiled my rage. My kids felt it. My husband felt it. I characteristically overreacted to most everything. I was stuck.

I found myself reading Fred's story in this chapter regarding his alcoholic dad. Fred would not forgive his dad because he needed to pay for the deep hurt he caused. Yes! That's it! For years I had felt that this pastor should pay for his sexual abuse. Yes, I should forgive him, but I couldn't release him until he paid. Then it happened. No bolt of lightening or bright flashes of light. But someone did pay—Jesus.

I knew that. Remember, I was raised in the church. But sitting in the quietness of the lobby, God drove that truth home to my heart. It became abundantly clear, for the first time, that I am not responsible to make him pay. That is God's business (Rom. 12:19).

With the Living Foundation Ministries phones ringing in the background, I prayed. I turned him over to God. I released him. The change was so immediate, I was even able to ask God to bless him if He wished.

Two more incredible things happened. First, I could now see He had a purpose for allowing this offense. Almost instantly I became focused. But something else happened. I began to see who God is and His purpose for coming.

Forgiveness for me was the doorway into the very heart of God. It's what Jesus' ministry on earth was all about. Forgiveness is the very core of being Christlike. These truths were there all the time. But my bitterness blinded me. It was as if my bitterness left me in the hands of tormentors all these years (Matt. 18:33–35).

Thanks, Fred. Your story put all the pieces together for me. You met God in the office. I met Him in the lobby. We both went home free to live again.

Fred's struggle to forgive highlights a very important truth: forgiveness is not foregoing punishment. It is transferring the offender over to God in our hearts, and saying good-bye, affirming our love or care for them, and then walking away free, purposing to live in love and liberty. It is a time to stop hating and start living.

◊

But this did not work for Nancy and for very good reasons.

Chapter 5

"They Don't Understand!"

Nancy *felt relieved* that she was normal. Knowing that even the most mature Christian does not totally forget either what they have done in the past or what was done to them was reassuring. But she was still stuck. She knew she should release her father for his physical and emotional abuse. But she could not.

I thought of Fred. He was not free to release his father until he finally understood how much Jesus had to suffer to pay for his dad's abuse. Maybe this was Nancy's need, too.

I asked Nancy gently: "If your father were here, and I laid him over my desk and began to whip him with a cat-o'-nine-tails, how many lashings would I have to give him before you would be willing to fully forgive him?"

I did not anticipate her response. God used Nancy's reaction and subsequent struggle to forgive to teach me a very valuable lesson. It has since been the key to unlocking the prison of bitterness for many other women.

THE GENDER GAP

Women? Why just women? Doesn't every biblical truth work for each gender equally? For there is "neither male nor female" in Christ (Gal. 3:28)! Yes, God's Word is always truth. However, God created male, and He created female (Gen. 1:27). They are different in many ways. You may be confronted with one of these differences when it comes to dealing with forgiveness. As noted earlier, men generally tend to act out their anger physically, while women tend to do it verbally. True, there are exceptions. But in my years of family counseling, rarely have I had a woman tell me she put her fist through the wall or tore off a door.

As I began the vivid description of beating her father on the back, Nancy's eyes grew wide and she began to cry out loud: "I don't want my father to be hurt." Confused, she continued, "I mean I do, but I don't."

It is this kind of response that confuses a male counselor, or even a husband. But when understood, it is very logical. Let me translate what Nancy just said. "I don't want my father to be hurt, but I do want him to feel what he has done to me. I want him to feel it, but I don't want him to have to experience it to feel it."

Understanding this single truth has revolutionized my counseling with women. Men usually do not seem to have the need to have their feelings understood as much as women do. It's one of those creation differences.

FORGIVENESS VS. UNDERSTANDING

When I speak in conferences and share these insights with a mixed audience, I can watch the eyes of women light up and the foreheads of men wrinkle conveying their perplexity. I hasten to share with the men that they can increase the quality of their relationship with their wives if they attempt to understand their feelings. Why? Because a woman usually does not want a detailed defense of her husband's mistakes, as much as she wants her husband to feel, understand, or just acknowledge the pain she felt when he hurt her. She is looking primarily for identification with her emotional pain—not an explanation or rationalization for her pain. If you cannot identify with her, then at least acknowledge to her how she feels.

Recently, I counseled a lawyer friend about rebuilding his marriage after an affair. He kept recounting to his wife his recent positive steps to correct behavioral patterns that led up to the affair. I interrupted him and strongly suggested that he stop explaining his behavior and start listening to her feelings. To do this I had him paraphrase back to her how he thought she felt, so that she could either confirm or correct her feelings. Then I turned to her and asked, "Do you want reasons and explanations for his behavior, or do you want him to attempt to enter in and understand how you feel?" "I want him to understand how I feel!" came her quick response.

This is the same thing Nancy wanted from her insensitive father. Nancy knew she probably would not forget the painful past events. But she was crying out for her dad to try to understand how she felt when he put her through the physical and emotional abuse.

Nancy turned to look at her friend who had come with her. "I've told Sheila that when my father dies, and I'm standing at the head of his casket, I want her to remind me that now, for the first time in his life, as he stands before the Lord, he will understand what he has done to me, and how it feels."

It was then that God stretched my own understanding to recognize another reason it is hard to forgive. The logic is, "I know I should forgive, but I can't forgive until I know he feels the deep pain I have endured." The offended person desires understanding of the emotional pain before she is able to grant forgiveness from the heart. Yet a distinction needs to be made between forgiving the offender and being understood by the offender. The offended party is obligated to forgive as soon as possible. But to be understood by the offender may take a very long time, if it is ever accomplished (Luke 23:34).

EMOTIONAL VS. PHYSICAL ABUSE

Perhaps one of the primary reasons emotional understanding is considered a major need, is found in answer to a question I have asked many seminar audiences: "Which is more painful, physical hurts or emotional hurts?" With women it is almost unanimous—emotional hurts. But not so with men. Why are men so slow to admit the reality of emotional pain? Simple. Our culture has taken away a man's created right to have emotions. Popular mottoes underscore this: "Real cowboys don't cry. Only sissies cry. Be a man about this."

One pastor tried to console an emotionally abused wife by saying, "At least he didn't hit you!" What was this well-meaning pastor reflecting? A false male belief that emotional hurts are not as painful as physical hurts, and that emotional abuse, while not acceptable, is really not a big deal.

But reality screams against this false concept. I have yet to have a man in my office who is in personal turmoil just because his dad beat him in the past. The most excruciating pain, once it is identified, is rejection, criticism, abandonment, lack of affection, non-affirmation, and never being able to measure up or please Dad. It is the absence of a relationship or friendship with Dad or guidance from him. This is not usually physical, but emotional abuse.

FEELING OUR PAIN

It is these kinds of issues that Dr. David Stoop sought to address in his book, *The Angry Man*. He explains that the primary source of a raging undercurrent of male anger is the diminishing influence of the father in a male's life. But he further explains that men cannot find peace because they cannot, or will not, bring their feelings to the surface and work through them.

Because a man tends to deny or avoid feelings, he expects his wife to do the same. He reasons: "If I don't feel it, you shouldn't feel it either." Now his wife is stuck with a cauldron of swirling emotions that she is not supposed to acknowledge or express. Therefore, she is unable to gain the freedom Christ provided through forgiveness. If she cannot feel them, she cannot identify them. If she cannot identify them, it stands to reason that she would not forgive them.

As Nancy glanced back to me, my eyes dropped to the floor. How could I tell her that her hope that her dad would finally realize how he hurt her when he got to heaven did not reflect accurate biblical theology?

Knowing what was about to take place, I carefully began to express to her that her dad may never—either here or in heaven—fully understand what he had done. I clarified to her that there is right now no condemnation awaiting her father in heaven (Rom. 8:1). God has not prepared a thirty-five-foot vista vision screen in heaven on which to replay all that a believer had done on earth. Her father is going to be there by grace (Eph. 2:8–9), not by any human effort (Titus 3:5–6). Her father's labor for Christ is going to be judged, and there will be a potential loss of rewards at the believer's judgment (1 Cor. 3:13–15). But the sin and shame have all been paid for in Christ (Heb. 12:2).

Nancy broke down and sobbed. I had just shattered her hope of release through her father's future understanding of her pain. She begged me to be wrong.

OUR GREAT HIGH PRIEST

Fortunately, at this point, I was reminded of the biggest asset a Christian counselor has: God's Holy Spirit. Instantly, He flashed a verse in my mind. It was then that I realized an application of a familiar truth that would be the key to set Nancy free.

I expressed to Nancy what I hoped would be good news. I asked her to describe what kind of High Priest we have as believers in Christ. Having had forty-plus years of listening to countless sermons and Sunday school lessons, she began to describe accurately what kind of High Priest we have. We began to quote in unison, "For we have not an high priest who cannot be touched with the feeling of our infirmities, but was in all points tempted like as we are, yet without sin" (Heb. 4:15 KJV). The Greek word for "touched" in this verse (*sympatheo*) is made up of two words that, when translated literally, mean "with" and "suffer." We get our word sympathy from it.

Then I shared the Amplified New Testament rendering of that verse: "For we do not have a High Priest Who is unable to understand and sympathize and have a shared feeling with our weaknesses."

It was important first for Nancy to begin to understand that Jesus does identify completely with our feelings (Heb. 4:15), and that He absorbs and responds to them personally.

I asked her if she could remember our Lord's words to Saul, who was stopped cold in his tracks by a blinding light while on his way to Damascus to arrest and persecute Christians. I began quoting the verse, and her lips began to mouth the words along with me. "Saul, Saul, why are you persecuting Me?" Notice he did not say, "Why are you persecuting Christians?"

Saul responded, "Who are You, Lord?" In answering Saul's question, He answered Nancy's question of emotional identification: "I am Jesus whom you are persecuting" (Acts 9:4–5). When Paul hurt Christians, Jesus felt it and responded to it. When Nancy's father hurt her, Jesus felt it. In this brief statement, Jesus explained how intimately we are attached to Him both spiritually and emotionally. Saul was directly and ultimately hurting Christ. This may have some bearing on why the Lord shared with Ananias that, although Saul would be an instrument of His to bear witness to His name before the Gentiles and kings, He would also show him how much he must suffer for His name's sake. And God must have put a special longing in Paul's heart for fellowship in suffering, because he expressed to the Philippians a desire that he "may know Him and the power of His resurrection and the fellowship of His sufferings" (Phil. 3:10).

Our Lord did not just begin to identify with us upon His assent into heaven. When describing the future judgment, He said that whoever feeds the hungry, gives drink to the thirsty, clothes the naked, visits the sick, to the extent that these things are done to the very least of these, it is done to Him (Matt. 25:35–40). Our Great High Priest continues to be a man of sorrows, and is very acquainted with the emotion of grief (Isa. 53:3)—His and ours.

This same need for shared feelings is to be reflected in the body of Christ: "If one member suffers, all the members suffer with it, and if one member is honored, all the members are honored with it" (1 Cor. 12:26). Apparently Paul understood that we too are to help absorb and attempt to understand the pain of another. For he strongly urged the Roman Christians "to rejoice with those who rejoice and weep with those who weep" (Rom. 12:15). This shared feeling and mutual acknowledgment of suffering goes two ways. God has entered into our pain. Now we have the privilege of entering into His pain. We do this when we innocently suffer and patiently endure it. This finds favor with God (1 Pet. 2:20).

Finally, I explained to Nancy that the Holy Spirit helps in our weaknesses and intercedes for us with groanings (deep emotions) too deep for words (Rom. 8:26). He reads our emotional pain and conveys it to the Father in a way we never could.

It took a few moments for all this to sink in. Nancy had to grieve the loss of the false belief that her father would ultimately understand his offenses. She then began to grow in the awareness that she did not have to go through life alone in the emotional understanding of her pain. She was comforted when she realized that Jesus knew, felt, absorbed, and shared with her in her pain, and friends, too, like Sheila, would enter into that pain with her.

I asked her if she would be willing to pray a simple prayer with me. She bowed her head. Briefly I had her pray:

Dear Heavenly Father, I thank you for the Lord Jesus Christ. I acknowledge that for years I have been focusing on my father and his need to understand me and my pain. I recognize now that he may never understand and feel the same agony he has caused me. I release him from this obligation to do so and forgive him for all the hurts he caused me. I now accept your compassionate understanding of my hurts. You knew them all along. Forgive me for my wrong focus. I now purpose to be comforted by Your understanding of my pain and rejoice in it. Thank you. Amen.

BITTER HOSTAGE

Withholding forgiveness until an offender understands or acknowledges the emotional pain they have inflicted is a subtle form of revenge. Why? Because it's hoping that the offender would hurt a little too, in order to understand. But this type of revenge robs you of your freedom and allows the offender to keep control of you.

During the Iranian crisis, President Carter stated that he would remain inside the confines of the White House until all the hostages were released. Apparently this played into the captors' hands. They knew they could control the President of the United States, the most powerful man in the world, through the hostages. President Carter unintentionally gave the captors the power to control him. In the same way, we give those who hurt us even more control by not releasing them. They control our thoughts, emotions, and decisions. But through forgiving their past offenses, we become free from their control in the present, even if they do not understand or acknowledge their sin and our pain (Luke 23:34).

◊

But what if I can't stand to be around them even if I were to forgive them? Does forgiveness mean I have to be friends with them? This was Rochelle's struggle, and a key insight gave her the freedom to do what she had refused to do for many years.

Chapter 6

"They Won't Even Acknowledge What They Did!"

N*ow Rochelle,*" her aunt sternly lectured, "you need to forgive your father like God forgives, and you should visit him, too."

Father. The very word triggered memories of a hot steamy jungle in Africa. Inside Rochelle, the voice of a frightened little girl in a panicked state begged her not to go near her dad. "He'll hurt me again," was her desperate plea.

The work of the mission seemed routine by all outward appearances. Lives were being introduced to Jesus Christ, and daily discipleship classes were making a deep change in the lives of the natives. This was the way it was by day. But by night, it was a very different story. Rochelle's father was an incestuous pedophile.

"Visit my father?" she questioned as her mind vividly replayed the immoral acts she was forced to participate in. Although she is now married and has three children of her own, each memory brings with it the fear of it recurring in the present. But this is not her deepest fear now. She fears for her own young children, the same ages as the little girl (herself) in her memories. "Sure, I know I should forgive my dad, but if forgiving him means I have to subject my children to his abuse, forget it!"

When Rochelle began to unravel her story to me, the major question haunting her was, "Does forgiveness mean I have to act towards those who hurt me just as if it never happened? Does forgiveness mean there should be an automatic restoration of relationship?" I didn't understand the full impact of her question until she shared her background with me.

Upon returning to the United States, the news of the alleged incest became known. Rochelle was ten by then. Her father was tried and declared innocent because of a lack of supporting evidence. At that time, children were not legally able to testify against their own parents. Ironically, it was because of this trial that the law was changed.

Even as an adult, Rochelle tried to get her father to own up to his sin. For Rochelle, it was never a case of memories she had repressed and later recalled—her memories never left. Although her mother denied the incest for fifteen years, she told a relative at Rochelle's wedding that she should not be wearing a white dress (a traditional symbol of moral purity). Finally, in broken regret, years later, she cried out to Rochelle and said, "What could I do? I couldn't leave your dad. How would we have survived? It's been hell living with him!"

Rochelle's questions about associating with her unrepentant father reflected her confusion over what the Bible teaches about two separate issues—forgiveness and trust.

SEEK PEACE

We are explicitly directed in Scripture to seek peace with

all men (Rom. 12:18). This peace is to be rigorously pursued (Heb. 12:14). We are to do everything within our capacity to bring about peace in relationships (Rom. 12:18). But what comes as a shock to many is that some people will never be reconciled to each other no matter how hard one may try or how much one forgives. For example, God has done everything He can do to reconcile the world to Himself, yet people still refuse to accept His provision for peace with Him through the sacrifice of His own Son. It is even God's will that none should perish (2 Pet. 3:9). But the sad reality is that many are going to die without establishing a personal relationship with God through His Son and will therefore spend eternity separated from Him (Rom. 6:23).

Like Rochelle's aunt, many have been led to believe that forgiveness is not complete until the severed relationship is restored. True, forgiveness can, and hopefully will, lead to restoration. But forgiveness and restoration of relationships are still two related but separate issues, much like forgiveness and trust.

NO CHANGE

Some people will not be reconciled to us, regardless of what we say or do. Our act of forgiving our offender may influence him, but not change him. True, each of us may either have, or know of, a personal story where an unrepentant offender melted into repentance because the other party took the first step toward forgiveness. I can personally attest to that with my own father.

I vividly remember a time when, as an adult, I stood before my father and acknowledged a wrong I had done as a child. My father broke down in a sob and acknowledged his own hurtful actions as an alcoholic for the first time in over twenty years. I had forgiven him years before, but it was the first time we both acknowledged the formerly unmentionables. Today I now give primary oversight for his care. This restored relationship would not have been possible apart from the scriptural tool of forgiveness.

But this is not the norm. Consider, for example, Jesus forgiving the Roman soldiers as they crucified Him. Though He cried out, "Father, forgive them, for they do not know what they are doing" (Luke 23:34), it did not stop His execution or establish a relationship with His executioners. In fact, they cast lots for His garments while He was making this plea to His Father (Matt. 27:35).

Steven experienced the same thing. While his persecutors hurled rocks, crushing his body, Steven cried out to God, "Lord, do not hold this sin against them." Even as he crumpled into a heap and died (Acts 7:60), there was no change, no repentance, and no reconciliation.

The apostle Paul seemed to confirm this deadlock when he identified attitudes and actions that will characterize people at the end of history as we know it. He explained to his disciple Timothy that in the last days difficult times will come: "For men will be lovers of self, lovers of money, boastful, arrogant, revilers, disobedient to parents, ungrateful, unholy, unloving." Then he declares, "irreconcilable" (2 Tim. 3:1–2). What does "irreconcilable" ("truce breakers") mean? The word "irreconcilable" is made up of two parts, the first means "no," and the second means "a libation" (drink offering). Literally, it means "without libation."

When two warring enemies came to negotiate a truce to end hostilities, each one of the belligerents would present a drink offering (libation) to seal the treaty or pact. This was the equivalent of the Native American custom of burying the hatchet. If one would not enter the peace pact by offering a drink offering, he was called implacable, or a truce breaker, or irreconcilable. Paul made it clear that an irreconcilable attitude would definitely characterize the end times. However, the "end time" mind set does not negate two important truths: First, reconciliation will always be God's priority for us (Matt. 5:23–24). And second, it is *our* responsibility to do all that is in our power to make it happen (2 Cor. 5:18).

NOT RESPONSIBLE

A major reason that people will be irreconcilable is very simple. Society today is characterized by a stubborn determination not to see or accept responsibility for its actions. We have a "no fault" society. No one is responsible for anything, or will even acknowledge participation in wrong or offensive behavior—regardless of how clear the evidence is. The paradox of this "no fault" society is its extreme need to blame and sue for almost anything in order to get something for almost nothing. The United States has the highest ratio of lawyers per capita of any industrialized nation in the world.

However, this "no fault" attitude is not a new development. God attempted to get Israel, while in Babylonian captivity, to recognize their responsibility for their behavior and to change. They insisted, "The way of the Lord is not right." God retorted, through the prophet Ezekiel, "Hear now, O house of Israel! Is My way not right? Is it not your ways that are not right?" (Ezek. 18:25).

Blame shifting started early with the first family—Adam and Eve. After Adam ate the forbidden fruit, God confronted him. Adam quickly responded to set the record straight: "The woman whom Thou gavest to be with me, she gave me from the tree, and I ate." In other words, "It is her fault, and if I may be so bold as to say, it is Your fault, too, God. If You had not given her to me, this difficult situation would not have happened" (Gen. 3:12).

LIGHTS OUT

Almost all of us have had the experience of trying to feel our way through a darkened room, only to stub our toe on an unseen obstacle. Groping in darkness is not only physically painful, but the darkness of denial can be both mentally and emotionally painful as well—if not to ourselves, then at least to others.

I asked Rochelle if she would be open to reading chapter one of First John. By the time she got to verse five, I slowed her reading down. Her voice was clear, though skeptical: "And [we] announce to you, that God is light, and in Him there is no darkness at all." Though beginning to look puzzled, she continued: "If we say that we have fellowship with Him and yet walk in darkness, we lie and do not practice the truth."

At this point, it was vital for Rochelle to understand a freeing truth regarding fellowship and association, especially with offenders. First of all, the emphasis of First John is on how to establish a basis for fellowship with God and one another. It is not about salvation.

Next, it is important to understand that God lives in the sphere of light that is defined as truth and reality. Therefore, if we do not live in the sphere of truth and reality, we are living in darkness. This darkness is defined as a "lie," or denial.

On the yellow notepad before her, I drew a line down

the center of the paper and wrote the words "light" on one side and "darkness" on the other. I drew a stick figure of her standing on the light side—in reality and truth. Then I drew a stick figure of her father standing in denial—in the darkness.

Remember, Rochelle had not gone to a counselor to recover her memories of sexual abuse—they were always present. Even years after the court trial, her father refused to acknowledge his sin. To this day he will not acknowledge what he did to her.

Then I asked her to read verse seven: "But if we walk in the light as He Himself is in the light, we have fellowship with one another, and the blood of Jesus His Son cleanses us from all sin."

"What is the basis of a relationship?" I asked her.

Tension was beginning to leave her face, she answered, "Truth. Reality."

"Is it God's fault we do not have fellowship with Him if we live in darkness, denial, or unreality?" Then came the pointed question: "Are you obligated to have fellowship with one who is living a lie, walking in darkness, and refusing to acknowledge or accept responsibility for his actions?"

In all her twenty-five years, no one had helped her make the important distinction between the basis for forgiveness and the basis for fellowship. When an offender refuses to recognize or acknowledge his sin, he is left in darkness. As a result, his fellowship and intimacy with the one he offended is greatly inhibited, whether it be in a family or a marriage relationship. The apostle Paul expressed this clearly with the following rhetorical questions: "For what partnership have righteousness and lawlessness, or what fellowship has light with darkness?" (2 Cor. 6:14).

Denial turns the light out. It is self-deception and is designed to be self-protective of our pride or to prevent further emotional pain. The Apostle John said, "If we say that we have no sin, we are deceiving ourselves, and the truth is not in us" (1 John 1:8). John's purpose in attacking the denial system is not to shame or condemn, but to establish a basis for fellowship in relationships. Then follows the clear process of correction, "If we confess our sins, he is faithful and just to forgive us our sins, and to cleanse us from all unrighteousness" (1 John 1:9 KJV).

I asked Rochelle what the pivotal word was in that verse. Her eyes squinted, she drew back, then she rolled them upward: "He'll never do it! My dad will never confess, or even acknowledge, his sin against me!"

AGREEING WITH GOD

As a young firebrand evangelist in Bible school, I used First John 1:9 to lead people to a personal relationship with Christ. I would have an unsaved person read this verse, and then tell him that if he acknowledged his sin to God, God would forgive him and save him. I still believe it is appropriate to use this verse in application in personal evangelism. However, this verse was not targeted by God for non-Christians, but for Christians, as indicated in verse three, ". . . that you also may have fellowship with us; and indeed our fellowship is with the Father" (1 John 1:3).

The basic meaning of the word *confession* here is important. First, it does not mean that we confess our sins to God to inform Him of something that He did not know. He is omniscient. God cannot be taught or informed. There is nothing He can learn. He has always known everything there is to know. The primary purpose of confession is to acknowledge to Him our behavior or attitude and agree with what He already knows, i.e., that it is sin. The key word here is *agree*. Confession is acknowledging and *agreeing* with God that what we did was wrong—it was sin.

I asked Rochelle what she would say if she caught one of her young sons slipping a candy bar into his pocket while waiting in the checkout line at the grocery store.

"Billy, what's in your pocket?"

"Nothing."

"What did you put in your pocket? Put your hand in your pocket and pull it out! How did that candy bar get in there?"

"I don't know."

"Son, I saw you put it in there just now."

His head drops. He's caught.

Now an outside observer might challenge her for putting her son through such an interrogation. Why do it if you already know what he did? The answer to that question is at the heart of the practice of confession. The mother wants her son to admit that he did what she saw him do and to confess and acknowledge it as wrong on his own. The purpose of confession is to see the sin as God sees it—not to plea-bargain it away or minimize it, but to acknowledge that it happened and that it was wrong. When we do that, God, out of His justice and faithfulness, forgives us, and we now are back to an open, free, growing relationship with Him. Our sin does not kick us out of the family, but it reduces or inhibits fellowship and intimacy with God *in* the family (Eph. 4:30).

These implications were revolutionary to Rochelle. She always knew she had to forgive her dad but she refused for fear she would have to associate with him and risk the possibility that he would repeat his perverted behavior on her own young children. Forgiveness was never intended to be the basis for a continued tolerance of sin (1 John 3:9).

FREE TO CHOOSE

Rochelle asked a pointed question. "Are you saying I can't see or visit with my dad?" This brings us to a very freeing concept. Because of circumstances beyond your control, you may find yourself in the presence of one you have forgiven but who is still in self-deceptive denial. You may have to casually *associate* with an unrepentant offender, but you are not obligated to *fellowship* with him if he continues to live the lie of denial. You are free to associate if you please. Many do. But it is important to know you are not obligated to. You are free to choose.

How does this square with what Jesus taught in the Sermon on the Mount in Matthew 5:23–24? "If therefore you are presenting your offering at the altar, and there remember that your brother has something against you, leave your offering there before the altar, and go your way; first be *reconciled* to your brother, and then come and present your offering."

The key words are "be reconciled." This is the only example of this compound word in the New Testament (Greek, *diallasso*). It is a command, and strongly suggests that we are to take the initiative. The verb, however, denotes mutual concession after mutual hostility (*dia*, "between two"). This word, however, is never used in reference to reconciliation between God and man. There is no such idea as "making it up" where God and man are concerned. God does not conceal anything. His character of holiness prohibits that. But in man-to-man relationships, each is able to make some basic concessions when appropriate to restore a relationship. Although it is God's command to be reconciled, it still takes two, not just one. This is why the apostle Paul said, "*If possible*, so far as it depends on you, be at peace with all men" (Rom. 12:18). The "if possible" indicates that, despite our best efforts to establish peace and fellowship, the other party may not cooperate with us, and reconciliation will not take place.

It is not our intent here to discuss all the ramifications of biblical separation (see 1 Cor. 5:9–13 and 2 Cor. 6:14). It is important, however, to understand that the believer does have some options here and that forgiveness and association are two separate issues.

FORGIVENESS AND CONSEQUENCES

Rochelle's reluctance to forgive her dad was also confused by another issue. I shared Becky's story with her.

When Becky discovered that her sister and brother-in-law were seriously abusing their children, she was really torn inside as to what to do. The sister repeatedly covered the abuse by explaining away the multiple bruises all over the children. Becky's parents defended the abusive behavior and told her to keep her nose out of their business. When Becky came to me and shared her inner conflict, I could see that she was confusing two issues. She did forgive her sister and brother-in-law for their hurtful behavior. But what about the continued abuse? Does forgiveness mean that we can release the offender from the practical or legal consequences of their behavior? If she was called to testify in court after reporting them to civil authorities, should she testify against them since she had forgiven them? If someone kills a family member of yours, do you have to forgive them? Yes! Can you absolve them from the consequences of their deeds? No! They have broken the law of the land, and it is the judicial system that has the responsibility to deal with the laws that were broken (Rom. 13).

When King David finally admitted his sins of adultery and murder, God forgave him and showed mercy to him rather than striking him dead for his sin. Nathan, the prophet, confirmed to David that his sin was forgiven (2 Sam. 12:13). Yet he also shared the consequences with him; namely, that "the sword would not depart out of his house" (12:10), and the baby conceived in adultery would die (12:14).

Forgiveness and consequences are separate issues. It is never appropriate to take personal revenge (Rom. 12:18). However, you are not obligated to shield the offender from the consequences of his sin either. How many parents come to realize too late that they should have let a wayward son spend a few nights in jail instead of quickly bailing him out only to repeat his behavior?

PROTECTION AND FORGIVENESS

The heart of Rochelle's inner turmoil was over forgiveness and her maternal instinct to protect her own children. It was one thing to have to casually associate with her father at family gatherings, but it was another issue to let the grandchildren spend unsupervised time with the grandparents. Releasing the offender does not mean you are not able or responsible to protect yourself or family from further harm. Again, forgiveness does not imply that you have to continue to be a doormat for their continued sin.

Rochelle's fears were well-founded. Since her father had not repented for his incest and received appropriate counseling, she was safe to conclude there had not been a change. My counseling files are full of religious grandfathers who molested their young grandchildren. Old age is not a sanctifier of the flesh. To put it another way, if my neighbor was to morally violate my daughter, would I have to forgive him? Yes! But would I have to send my daughter next door to prove I had forgiven him? No way! Why? Because forgiveness and consequences, as well as trust, are separate issues. Could I testify against him? Yes! For the sake of revenge? No! For the sake of justice? Yes! (Rom. 13:4)

Linda's struggle came about twenty years later. Her son knew what his grandfather did to his mother. She did not poison her son with bitterness toward her father. When her son was in college, he indicated a desire to have a relationship with his grandfather. Linda felt betrayed. Her father never acknowledged the incest. Her mother did. Now her son wanted to spend time with him. Protection is no longer an issue. He could take care of himself. What I had to clarify for Linda was that the incest was her and her dad's issue—not the grown son's. She had to let him deal with his grandfather on his own terms. It was not a matter of loyalty as much as it was responsibility. The son was now responsible to deal with the grandfather on an adult-to-adult basis.

A similar situation occurs when a child wants to have a relationship with a non-custodial divorced mom or dad. Often the children are made to choose sides. The spouse with primary custody may be hurt to think that the child does not see, understand, or accept the hurt caused by the divorce. But a wise parent will work to build appropriate loyalty with the children towards the other parent even in a difficult divorce situation.

FORGIVENESS AND TRUST

The final issue for Rochelle to understand was that forgiveness and trust, as we mentioned earlier, are two separate issues. We are commanded by God to forgive an offender before the sun sets (Eph. 4:26) and even to forgive many times a day (Luke 17:4). However, after an offender is forgiven, trust has to be earned to be rebuilt. Forgiveness is to be granted immediately, but trust takes time to establish. Forgiveness is granted; trust is earned. Even after warring tribes or clans symbolized their recently established peace by burying not one but two hatchets (or tomahawks), they set up geographic boundaries—they put distance between each other. Declarations of peace did not always accompany trust. That took time.

Usually, the deeper the genuine repentance by the offender, the sooner the trust is rebuilt in the offended. Some, indeed, will put on an appearance of repentance and sorrow over their past deeds. But over time the reality of true repentance and the fruit of repentance may allow the wounded one's spirit to open again to love in the freedom of forgiveness.

Rochelle shook her head. "To think," she said reflectively, "I've carried this pain needlessly for so long, thinking it was so hard to forgive." I asked if she was open for me to lead her in a prayer to forgive and release her dad. She nodded her head. The tears flowed and her freedom began.

Rochelle's dad wouldn't acknowledge his sin, but Amber's grandfather *couldn't*—he was deceased.

DECEASED AND FORGIVEN

Amber was angry at men. Her divorce was final three weeks before she came to see me. It was very difficult for her to have good relationships, especially with men.

In junior high she had uncontrollable rage. In high school she got pregnant and dropped out. Then her world fell apart—her grandpa died when she was sixteen. She hated God for that.

It was not long until she was able to share that she, like Rochelle, had been molested as a child—by her grandpa. He was her best friend. They did a lot of fun things together. Then there was the dark side.

When I delicately approached the subject of forgiveness, she said she knew she needed to forgive him but she couldn't do it because he was dead. How do you forgive a dead person? What good would it do?

First, I explained as I did with Fred, that forgiveness is primarily to benefit us. Secondly, God lives outside of time. There is no past, present, or future with Him. Time is a created thing for a created people. Therefore, to God the events are always today. Her memories and emotions are as fresh today as they were over eighteen years ago. True, Grandpa cannot acknowledge his sin, but we can let God acknowledge them for him.

Amber was able to put Grandpa into the Jesus jail. The list of offenses exceeded a dozen. Then I asked her if she would do a special project—write a letter to Grandpa and give him the gift of forgiveness. She agreed! I was not emotionally prepared for what I was going to hear the day she read me her letter to Grandpa. I was reaching for a Kleenex halfway through it. It is the hallmark of forgiveness letters.

I asked permission to share it with the greater Living Foundation Ministries family. It was Christmas time. She said she would be happy to. She entitled it, "A Gift for Grandpa." It is included in this book as a personal encouragement to all of those whose offenders are not able to acknowledge their sin against you. But that will not stop you from being free. I warn you, it is a two-hanky letter.

"A GIFT FOR GRANDPA"

Dear Grandpa,

I am writing this letter to share with you a few changes that have taken place in my life. But first of all I want to tell you thanks for all that you have done for me. You gave me a lot of special memories. For instance, the times you shaved, whipped up your cream, and painted your face. I was always fascinated by all that cream. Then there were times you would let me put the cream on your face. Sometimes I would put the cream on me, but you would never let me shave it off my face. Then there were the times of washing and waxing your car with you to make it shiny and new looking. Sometimes we would splash and play in the water. I want to thank you for loving me and being my friend when there seemed to be no others.

I also want you to know I am on a spiritual journey, working toward inner healing with the Lord Jesus in my heart. But I am having trouble in the area of the things you did to me when I was a little girl. So, through my struggle to help me move on in my healing, I want to give you a gift, the most special gift I could give to you. That gift, Grandpa, is forgiveness. I want to explain to you what kind of forgiveness it is. My gift of forgiveness to you is for all the violations done against me by you when I was growing up. I will explain.

I want to forgive and release you for violating me by using my body for your own sexual pleasure.

I want to forgive and release you for prematurely stimulating my sexual feelings, something I never understood before as a child.

I want to forgive you and release you for the mistrust you developed in me, training me not to let anyone be too close to me for fear of being hurt.

I want to forgive and release you for making me feel so ashamed when I did nothing wrong.

I want to forgive and release you for setting me up to falsely blame myself for something I could not control or make stop as a little child.

I want to forgive and release you for the anger you developed inside me towards you.

I want to forgive and release you for the hate and fear of men that you instilled in me, even towards my dad, whom I now love with all my heart.

I want to forgive you and release you for making me feel as if I deserved the pain from what you were doing to me while growing up.

I want to forgive you and release you for instilling insecurity in me, which I still struggle with. But I am coming to realize that I am someone whom God made special and have a purpose to fulfill in this world for the Lord Jesus Christ.

I want to forgive and release you for the confusion of not knowing if what you were doing was right or wrong and also for not understanding the feelings I had from what you were doing. [Author's note: the Hebrew word for *incest* means "confusion."]

I want to forgive you and release you for deceiving and lying to me and threatening me not to tell by saying I deserved it. If I deserved it, why? What had I done? I was an innocent child, confused into believing that what you were doing was allowed. (I didn't understand any other way.)

I want to forgive you and release you for shattering my dreams for a happy marriage with someone to really love me. You changed me from what I really was to someone I didn't know, and I didn't understand what was happening to me. But I have faith that through all of this, with God by my side, there is someone special out there for me who will understand what I have gone through and will love me regardless.

The most important thing I want to forgive you and release you for is the distorted picture of God you gave me. You made me blame Him for the sin you were committing which was not His fault. As a child I could not understand how a God who loved me, and in the Bible said He was there for me and would protect and guide me, could let something like this happen. Now I know that it was not His fault, and He was there all the time for me. But as a scared little girl, I probably did not listen when He tried to talk to me because I did not believe what He had to say.

Grandpa, now that I have completed this part of the journey and transferred you over to the Lord through forgiveness, I want to make a promise in my heart that I will never bring this up against you again.

It is time to draw this letter to a close and say good-bye. Before I do, I want to thank you again for all the good memories you have given me. I will always cherish those times. Now that I feel better about myself and can accept what has happened to me, I can really say I know what it means to love you through the eyes of the Lord.

Amber

Letters poured into our office requesting reprints or permission to copy. It underscored for me the number of dear people who know *I Should Forgive, But. . .* and can't feel the full release when their offenders are deceased.

◊

For Dan, however, it was not a matter of his dad acknowledging his abuse. Dan couldn't care less. Rather, it was the daily reminders Dan lived with that prevented him from releasing his dad.

Chapter 7

"I'm Living with the Memories!"

Forgive? Are you kidding?! Every waking moment of my life I live with the damage my dad did to me. You see this scar? My dad threw a bottle at me because I didn't answer quickly enough. Sure he was drunk, but it still hurts. But it's not just the physical scars. I can't get into a deep sleep. I live in constant fear my dad will come into my room sometime in the night and start beating on me for something he didn't like. Years after I left home, I still have these recurring nightmares. Emotionally I can't cry, but I can spring into a rage over nothing. I keep people at a distance, even my wife and kids. I'm a basket case and you want me to just 'let go'? I know I should, but I can't. I can't get away from him—he's everywhere!"

Dan's response is sadly typical. For many, it is easier to put an offender in the Jesus jail and go on when the painful reminders are less severe.

As Dan sat in my office one evening, he unfolded five computer-generated pages of incidents of his father's abuse. My mind went back to an article in the newspaper about Charles Rosenberg who doused his eleven-year-old son with kerosene and ignited it to keep his estranged wife from winning a custody battle. Many surgeries later, his son could carry on a routine life but was grossly disfigured. He hated his father and never wanted to see him after he was released from prison. For the son, the mirror was a daily reminder of his emotionally disturbed father's actions.

THE LOGIC

Each of these friends are living with consequences. But Dan's reasoning spoke for all of them: "I know I should forgive, but I can't because I'm still living with the consequences." This logic implies that if there are no consequences, then forgiveness would not be so hard. But the real issue is this: I refuse to accept upon myself the consequences of the hurts someone caused me in the past; therefore, I refuse to grant forgiveness in the present.

TAKING CONTROL

To see Dan outwardly, one would think he had everything. He was college educated, upwardly mobile in his career, and handsome. But inwardly, he felt powerless. I asked him if he had ever heard of the serenity prayer: "Lord, grant me the serenity to accept the things I cannot change, the courage to change the things I can, and the wisdom to know the difference." One of the keys in this simple prayer is ". . . and the wisdom to know the difference." Difference? Yes. It would take a great deal of wisdom to distinguish between the things I can change and have control over and the things that are beyond my control to change.

The first step in Dan's spiritual recovery was to take back

control of those things that were under his control. I had him make two columns on his notepad. Then I asked him to write down his mental list of the continuing consequences in the left column. When he completed the list, I suggested that we go over each item and determine if there was anything that was under his control to change or correct. Then I had him designate those things that were totally out of his control.

This step is important, because usually these two concepts are not distinguished, and the unchangeable consequences blur our ability to change or correct the ones that we actually can correct or improve.

One of the very first things he listed in the left column was the physical abuse. While pointing to it on the pad and glancing up with a glaring eye, he said, "I'd like to see you change that!" That was simple. What is sown is sown. We can't undo it. Rewriting it does not change the reality of it. But I challenged him: "What do you think you could change regarding this history?" He looked bewildered. What meaning did he put on his father's abuse? What was his response to all these events? How much control did he give to all those events? I clarified to Dan that while we cannot change history, we can change the meaning, value, and control that the events of history have on us. I shared my story:

Years ago my father abandoned my mother with three sons. My alcoholic father chose his wine, women, and song over his family. That is history. But as a child I put a meaning on his abandonment and concluded that my dad must not love me. That response led to my feeling that I was not lovable, and the net result was that I felt that no one could love me. Later I resurrected this false core belief and examined its roots. I had to go back and change the meaning of my childhood memory of the historical event of my father's abandonment. In adulthood I realized that he was out of control and addicted to alcohol. My father's desertion was not a love issue; it was an addiction issue. I had to change the misperception that there was something innately wrong with me as a young boy that caused my father's addiction and ensuing abandonment. That myopic view of a child was just that—a child's perception of childhood events. He didn't just abandon *me*, but the whole family. As an adult I can see this and change the childhood misperception.

Then I tackled my feelings of being unloved. I listed my feelings about why no one could love me. Then I listed all the Scriptures that revealed truth contrary to these feelings. Why? Because truth is the first weapon in our spiritual arsenal [Eph. 6:14] against misbeliefs. It was at this point that I began to take control of my past and to reduce the control the past had on me.

"What does that have to do with forgiveness?" challenged Dan.

Everything! It meant that I had gotten back a lot of the power I felt I had lost. I had felt like a victim. But by correcting my thoughts, I became a victor; yes, more than a victor (Rom. 8:37).

Again, you can't change your history. Many of the consequences can't be changed, and you have to live with them either way. But you do have the power to choose how you are going to live with them. Your options are at least two:

1) bitterness and bondage (being out of control)
2) forgiveness and freedom (being under control)

BITTERNESS AND BONDAGE

After thirty-five years of people-helping, I never cease to be amazed at the inverted thinking of bitter people. For most, their deep hurts have left them feeling overwhelmingly helpless, because they felt overpowered in their developmental years. The result of being overpowered was a feeling of helplessness. So they determined, out of bitterness, that they would always be in control. That way they could end or reduce any further personal hurts or losses from the outside. This logic is crazy. The reasoning goes like this: "I'm not going to forgive because I want to be in control so I won't feel so helpless again." What a joke! They think being bitter is being in control, when in reality they are being controlled by bitterness! I have never met a person who had to be in control of everything and everybody that was not also bitter and dreadfully fearful. Because of a fear of being out of control on the inside, they mistakenly believe that they can get some self-control by controlling people, places, and things on the outside. Some perfectionists are classic examples of this pattern.

Betty felt the romance was out of her thirty-two-year marriage. Her major complaint was that her husband always had to have complete control of everything and became angry when he was not. I inquired about his background, especially his relationship with his father. She indicated that he had had a love/hate relationship with his dad. Bingo! Bitterness! He loved his dad for being his dad but hated what Dad did to him.

Dan was a control freak. Panic would set in if change confronted him; it was something he could not control. His controlling ways were only one manifestation of his perfectionism. His environment had to be perfect—car, home, and office. His perfectionism occupied his mind so that he would not re-experience the feelings of anger and the deep-seated bitterness that was ultimately in control of him. The apostle Peter discovered this in Simon.

Peter rebuked Simon, who had tried to purchase the authority to lay hands on people to receive the Holy Spirit. More authority meant more power and more control. Peter responded to his request by saying, ". . . for I see that you are in the gall of bitterness, and in the bondage of iniquity" (Acts 8:23). Simon did not have a clue as to his own spiritual and mental state. For all he knew, he was free to try to leverage himself in the marketplace of the healing arts by trying to purchase the Holy Spirit. He did not know there was a deep wound in his own spirit, resulting in bitterness. This bitterness opened him up to bondage (fetters) to some kind of sin that was out of control, perhaps an addiction.

Many addictions have their root in bitterness, coupled with fear—especially the fear of abandonment. An unforgiving heart is a life out of control and in bondage. It is still open to manipulation by many things, including the circumstances the one in bondage is trying to avoid.

FORGIVENESS AND FREEDOM

Those still in the bondage of bitterness usually develop a synthetic system to live by that is a substitute for true freedom. Freedom is different. Freedom is a *choice*. Hurt is inevitable, but bitterness is optional. Bitterness is a choice. Freedom is the result of taking control of one's own life. In freedom I am not an out-of-control victim, but an under-control victor.

"But I can't do that," protested Dan. "It's just not in me."

"Good!"

"Good?" he said in amazement.

"Yes! Before we determine whether or not we can do it, let's determine if God wants us to do it."

Why? Because, you and I can do anything God expects of us through Christ who gives us the strength to do it (Phil. 4:13). What power! What control! What freedom! Jesus injects you with the power and desire to process any deep hurt that will give you back control of your life. Why? Because the ninth fruit of the Spirit is self-control (Gal. 5:23). When we are clean from the bitterness, God's Spirit can fill us and through His Spirit give us the real self-control we desire. Now that is freedom!

MY WAY, HIS WAY

We live in an age of individualism and of doing things "my way." This same mindset finds its way into practical theology. I frequently hear, "I know what God says, *but . . .*," and the person goes on to say how they are going to do what God says, but in their own way. This individualism, which is in reality a rewriting of God's way, can be very devastating personally. King Saul learned this the hard way. God asked Saul to destroy the Amalekites. He did destroy most of them, but he spared the best sheep and oxen under the pretense that he would sacrifice them to God (1 Sam. 15:15). The prophet Samuel firmly rebuked Saul for his incomplete obedience. He further stated that it is better to obey God by following all of His instructions than to come up with creative ways to sacrifice for God (1 Sam. 15:22). To fail to do this is disobedience. And, for the record, "his way" ultimately killed him. It was the sword of an Amalekite that finally did Saul in (2 Sam. 1:1–10).

Dan, in no uncertain terms, informed me: "I have dealt with my dad in my own way." I could imagine that any similarity between Dan's way and God's way was purely accidental.

ACCEPTING THE CONSEQUENCES

Dan was clueless as to what God's way of forgiveness is. The apostle Paul gives us a hint of what genuine forgiveness includes: ". . . forgiving each other, just as God in Christ also has forgiven you" (Eph. 4:32). How did Christ forgive us? He took the offenses of others and put them on Himself. Peter helps fill in the picture: ". . . for by His wounds you were healed" (1 Pet. 2:24). Jesus absorbed in Himself both the verbal and physical abuse of His tormentors. If we are going to forgive God's way, we, too, must be willing to take upon ourselves the pain and loss of others' offenses, *and accept the consequences for them.* Now you know why Jesus cried out so loudly, "My God, My God, why hast Thou forsaken Me?" (Mark 15:34). He was accepting on Himself the abandonment and loss that came when He took our sin upon Himself. Again, this explains how far God had to go to forgive. The cost was excruciatingly painful.

Dan's way of forgiveness seemed to be a mental gymnastic maneuver. On the one hand it gave intellectual assent to forgive, but on the other hand refused to take on the full consequences of his dad's sin and live in freedom with those consequences. Dan failed to understand that forgiveness is not just granting release for an offense. That's the easy part. Forgiveness is also accepting upon ourselves the full consequences of the other person's offense against us. That's the hard part. Some consequences can be changed. But others, by God's grace, we live with. We have to live with them either way. The only choice we have is how. We can live with them in acceptance, or in bitterness. Dan's system rejected the consequences, and as a result he became controlled by them. All the while, his whole quality of life was deteriorating. If his system was working for him, why was his wife ready to leave him, his son in rebellion, and he himself on the doorstep of a mental breakdown?

"I WAS SET UP"

Frequently I hear parents of teenagers express how upset they are to see their children make so many bad choices—drugs, sex, delinquency, bad friends, dropping out of school, abandonment of responsibility, etc.

I have spent literally hundreds of hours listening to parents pour out their hearts to me about their children. Then I have listened to teens describe that same home situation. Without fail, the descriptions are along these lines: there is fighting and yelling, favoritism, neglect, workaholism, overt and constant criticism, disregard for the child's feelings, overprotection, authoritarianism, and no affection, affirmation, or "I love you"s. Usually when parents stress the fact that their kids are making wrong choices, they reflect some selective amnesia, denial, or outright ignorance. When counseling these kinds of adolescents now in adulthood, we can easily trace the way they were set up for their poor choices.

Brenda, at sixteen, was living with a man almost twice her age. Her father was aloof, critical, demeaning, and very religious. Because of the love vacuum created by her father, she sought out immoral relationships with older men to fill the void. This choice was wrong. It was sin. It was displeasing to God. Her parents railed on her poor choice and the fact that she was away from God. But if God had been consulted, He would have clarified His pattern of parent-child restoration which He explained at the conclusion of the Old Testament: " . . . and he [Elijah] the prophet will restore the hearts of the fathers to their children and the hearts of the children to their fathers." The seriousness of the failure of this pattern is punctuated by these concluding words, " . . . lest I come and smite the land with a curse" (Mal. 4:6).

After meeting with Brenda, we were able to trace her behavior back to her home. She was honest when she listed her hurts. Then we led her in a prayer of forgiveness for her parents. But now, what about her choices?

One of the most important things for Brenda to realize was that she now had power over her past. She no longer had to satisfy unmet childhood needs through relationships with older men. When she forgave those who set her up for her poor choices, she was then able to take back the power and no longer be controlled by those offenses from her home environment. The key element in Brenda's forgiveness was *acceptance*. She had to accept the many losses she had as a child, grieve those losses, and accept the fact that she was going to have to learn to do some things differently. This is what Dan refused to do. Why? Because it meant admitting that his system was not working and that he would have to abandon it. He would then have to accept God's procedure, which included accepting the unchangeable consequences and taking responsibility for changing the ones that could be changed.

Forgiveness not only means releasing the offender, but

realizing afterward that it may result in the need to do a lot of relearning. We have to understand what mental distortions took place. We must put away the lies from these early developmental distortions (1 Cor. 13:11) and replace the distortions with truth and acceptance. Then, we must purpose to live a life of self-control, empowered by the Holy Spirit. It is our responsibility to "renew our mind" (Rom. 12:2); that is, to change the way we think and feel, or the way we were set up to think and feel. Part of the consequences of another's sin against us will be the distortion of our own thinking. We can take back that power and no longer be controlled by "set up" thinking. We are no longer under the "I can't help myself" thinking. We can choose to live with the "I can help myself with the biblical tools God gives" attitude that results in freedom. This releasing has not been easy for many down through the years. As warring tribes went their separate ways after burying two tomahawks in the sun-warmed earth, they had to relearn how to live without fear, anger, and revenge.

TREASURE FROM TRASH

It was now time to ask the hard question: "Dan, have you ever seen any benefit to you today from what your father did years ago?"

"Benefit! You must be joking! My dad trashes my childhood—my whole life—and you think I can see any benefit from that?" His head just shook from side to side and his eyes fixed on the floor. "Okay, you're the 'shrink.' You have all the answers. How am I supposed to see any good? I'm a mess!"

Dan was like some individuals who seek out Christian

counseling thinking there is some sort of special aura surrounding the counselor—that counselors have it all together throughout life and are able to dispense unending wisdom from a pain-free life. This could not be further from the truth. More often than we like to admit, most of us have come from a background of serious trauma and family dysfunction. In fact, that is often the impetus for our choice of vocational counseling or ministry.

By now I had built a degree of acceptance with Dan, and he became teachable. I asked him if he recalled the story of my alcoholic father. Because of his alcoholism and its effects on the family, I had sustained a lot of losses. But I reaped some benefits as well. I firmly believe that much of my empathy, tempered by an understanding of God's mercy and grace, can be directly attributed to the negative experiences I sustained as a child and adolescent.

My personal freedom from the debilitating control of the past was due in part to my new perspective of that history. I did not rewrite it to make it all come out right. But I was able to see some benefits from the past that are helpful to me today. Dan only saw the trash. He was not yet able to see any treasure or value in it. He had not recycled his past and converted the trash into treasure.

I was surprised to see in a national news magazine a report of how entrepreneurs in California were taking tabs from soft drink cans and making earrings with them. Also women were sporting their new purses fashioned of recycled tires. It was hard for me to think anyone would pay money for these fashion objects, but they were! I shared that bit of news along with my personal story regarding my father. Dan remained skeptical. I began by asking: "Have you ever given thanks to God for what has happened to you?" I think Dan thought I had lost it by then. But I continued to press with a difficult verse to practice: "In everything give thanks; for this is God's will for you in Christ Jesus" (1 Thess. 5:18). Notice it does not say "feel" thankful—it says "give thanks." "Give thanks" means that, by an act of our will, we are to thank God "in everything."

His wide eyes said it all. "Why? Why should I?"

That's a legitimate question. The answer is the key to turning trash into treasures. After I forgave my dad and was able to thank God for my heritage, I began to be bombarded by the benefits and purposes for all my suffering. Giving thanks to God opens the door of our spirit to receive His purposes for our pain (2 Cor. 1:6). Even now God continues to show new insights and benefits from my past that are helping hundreds of people today through the LFM ministry. Would I have chosen that past? No way! Did I want it? No! But while those events were out of my control, understanding the meaning and benefits of them are under my control. I can say without a doubt that I am a better pastor, teacher, people-helper, husband, and father because of my processed past—not in spite of it. I am rich in blessings today because of the poverty of my past. Doors have opened beyond my wildest imagination. I appreciate things today that I would not have, had I not gone through it.

I shared with Dan that I do not just live with the consequence of another's sin against me. I take control and I choose to forgive. I choose to accept the things I cannot change and to change the things I can. Victims become victors when they can see the value of their losses. Dan was not even trying to see any benefits from the past. All he wanted to do was make up for it today.

MAKE UP FOR THE LOSS

Dan continued to confuse two additional issues in forgiveness—of accepting consequences versus attempting to make up for the loss. Some have called this compensation or personal repayment for the loss. We are going to look at this from two perspectives: first, compensating one's self for losses experienced, and second, attempting to compensate others for any losses we may have caused them.

"I OWE IT TO MYSELF"

One of the distinct characteristics of one who is refusing to accept the loss as a part of forgiveness is over-compensation, or maintaining an "I-owe-it-to-myself" attitude. It is a form of repayment for a wrong endured and a deferment of accepting the loss. True, it is morally right for one who has offended you to make any restitution, if that is physically possible. If someone stole a hundred dollars from you, you need to forgive them whether the restitution is made or not. But restitution is just as vital a part of reconciliation as forgiveness is. Making restitution or compensation is morally right. However, when an offender is not able to do so, either physically or emotionally, the one offended might be tempted to compensate himself in order to offset the personal pain of loss. Or, he might be tempted to counterbalance the loss so he won't have to feel or face the reality of his loss. This develops into the reasoning that "I owe it to myself for all that I have endured! It's now my turn to live. I can make amends to myself with this indulgence." The tragedy of this is that it is not born out of forgiveness and peace but out of anger and bitterness and a continual sense of inner turmoil. It only deepens the pain and delays genuine freedom through biblical acceptance.

There is a major difference between living a new life of liberty in Christ through forgiveness and living a primarily selfish life out of anger, resentment, and self-indulgence. You may not have been able to play and have fun in childhood. But now, in Christ, you are free from the emotional bondage through forgiveness and you can laugh and play in many wholesome ways. However, an "I owe it to myself" lifestyle is usually achieved at someone else's expense. Affairs by both men and women are just one popular way of gaining a temporary relief from loss. An obsession with adult toys (boats, cars, houses, clothes, etc.) is usually a vain attempt to fill the hole in our soul and anesthetize ourselves from the feeling of painful losses. And this is exactly what Dan did. He would buy a new Corvette as fast as the new model could be introduced.

GUILTY COMPENSATION

But what if we caused the pain and want to compensate others—to try to make it up to them for past offenses?

King David lost a son by trying to make amends to his family for the guilt he still felt years after his affair with Bathsheba, even though he officially made her one of his wives and raised the children she bore him as royal heirs. The guilt he felt over this past affair may have kept David from rendering judgment when his daughter, Tamar, was raped by her half brother Amnon. Because David did not take action, as would have been mandated by Jewish law for such a crime, Absalom, Tamar's brother, took revenge for the assault against his sister (2 Sam. 13). Absalom held a party and had his servants kill Amnon during the height of merriment.

There are indications in the story that show David may have sensed that something potentially evil was up, but ignored that subtle warning because he felt he had to make up for all the past family pain. David may not have been able to act responsibly because of his false guilt. False guilt? Yes. David confessed his sin after he was confronted by Nathan the prophet and received forgiveness. David was no longer worthy of blame (guilt).

Before we confess our sin to God, we are legitimately worthy of blame or guilt. But if we confess our sin to God, we are forgiven and cleansed from all unrighteousness (1 John 1:9). If we continue to feel guilty, it is now false guilt. True guilt and false guilt feel the same. Therefore, the guilt feeling must be tested with truth. If guilt continues after sin is confessed and forgiven, then it is false guilt. However, if it has not been confessed and forgiven, the continued guilt is legitimate. It is appropriate to have a sense of sadness for our past actions. That is one of the important steps of working through grief. However, sadness and guilt are two very different emotions and must be responded to differently.

False guilt may cause a parent or spouse to act irresponsibly in order to make up for losses the child or spouse has suffered as in a divorce. Parents may have a hard time saying no to children when it is appropriate. They may feel the need to overprotect or overindulge, thinking they have to make up to the children for losses that they have experienced through a divorce. Somehow divorced parents feel that it is their responsibility to repay children for pain caused by the divorce. Parents believe that children have experienced enough losses. They may feel they have to make up for the child's losses financially, or by lenient behavior. However, the loss must be grieved by both the parent and child—not covered up with "things" and further parental permissiveness or indulgence. Overcompensation to make up for loss, whether ours or someone else's, usually short circuits the full forgiveness process of living with the loss in freedom and acceptance.

OVERCOMPENSATION

The memories of the Great Depression have all but faded from history. As a boy, I would often hear what it was like to experience the abrupt loss of everything and to have very little to eat—to say nothing of the bread lines. Great losses were experienced in the crash of 1929. However, out of their bitterness some of the survivors purposed that their children would never suffer the same loss or humiliation. After World War II, the Baby Boomers were born. Depression era parents said in their hearts, "My kids will never have to go through what I did. I'm going to give them everything I never had. They will never suffer lack." Result? The rebellion of the '60's. The flower children repudiated all that hard-earned security, materialism, and core values, and our nation plunged into an adolescent hedonism. This, in my opinion, is the "gift" of parents who were trying to make up for the loss of the Great Depression. Money and security, advancement and corporate mobility, were achieved at the expense of relationships.

I was a youth pastor in Southern California in the late '60's. I never met a genuine hippie who was not alienated by one or both parents. The young men felt betrayed by their fathers who gave them everything but themselves. Young women with empty father love-buckets were searching to get them filled through sex. Girls gave sex to get love; boys used sex to feel like a man. Because there was little or no peace in the home, the flower children tried to fix the world and, thus, vicariously fix their home. Much of this is the legacy of overcompensation for the Great Depression and the bitter fruit of overcompensation.

Anthony was a very successful psychiatric nurse by the age of thirty-seven, but his marriage was a mess. To top it all off, he was a very dependent person. As we explored his family background, he repeatedly reminded me that he came from a very good home. When asked about his father, "great guy" was his only response. "He gave me anything I needed." Then his countenance abruptly changed and a combination of anger and tears burst forth. "Every time I had a problem he would just give me money. He never talked to me; he just gave me more money." Startled, he shook his head and said, "Where did that come from?" Where it always was, just below the surface. Money was security and solved all problems. His elderly father was a teenager in the Great Depression. He, like others, tried to fix his own pain by overcompensating his children so they would not experience the same hardships. He wanted to avoid his own painful memories by preventing his children from experiencing need because that would trigger his own past painful memories.

Numbing our pain with things, drugs, relationships, jobs, hobbies, or adult toys does not bring acceptance. It's only a temporary anesthetic that, in time, will wear off. Then we will still have to begin where we left off—learning to forgive and to accept a "forgiven scar."

"I'm Living with the Memories!"

◊

Shirley was attempting to numb her losses her way—in immoral relationships. But she thought she had an additional problem—she could not forgive herself.

Chapter 8

"I Can't Forgive Myself!"

Sadness and shame just radiated from her downcast eyes. Guilt, remorse, and shame from an immoral past had taken its toll. She had three children from three different fathers, and now she was pregnant with a fourth. I asked Shirley if she had ever confessed these moral failures to God and sensed that He had forgiven her. She nodded, but her face still reflected a deep sense of regret and shame. "But," she gradually disclosed, "that's not the issue. I . . . I guess I can't forgive myself."

"Please don't waste your time trying," I said gently. Startled, she blinked, and looked up with puzzled disbelief.

Self-forgiveness can be one of the most confusing aspects of the issue of forgiveness. In reality, those who feel the need to "forgive themselves" make forgiveness harder than it really is. Because of this confusion between self-forgiveness and God's forgiveness, it is difficult, and for some impossible, to gain the heartfelt release that comes from experiencing genuine forgiveness from God.

Both theologians and therapists have grappled with the necessity, duty, or appropriateness of self-forgiveness. It is not taught, recommended, or illustrated in Scripture. That in itself does not make it wrong. Surprisingly, neither is the procedure of "asking forgiveness" found in Scripture. True, Jesus declared that, if a brother has something against us, we should stop, leave, and first be reconciled to our brother (Matt. 5:23–24). Here, however, as in other places, He focuses on the end (reconciliation), and not the procedure (asking for forgiveness). I personally believe asking for forgiveness is a legitimate discipline, even though it is not specifically taught or illustrated in Scripture.

One could say, "Did not the deeply indebted slave ask the king to forgive his overwhelming debt?" The king did forgive his debt! This was part of an illustration of forgiveness to Peter, who inquired how many times he was to forgive (Matt. 18:21–35). Yet a closer examination of the passage reveals that, yes, the slave humbled himself, pleaded for patience, and promised full payment, but he did not ask that the debt be forgiven. Restitution or repayment is not forgiveness, although both are biblical practices.

The fine points of theological faith and practice were not at the root of Shirley's need. The issues that were confusing her led her to a perceived need to forgive herself. I have seen this many times. However, after clarifying the issues biblically for many people, the need to forgive themselves becomes a moot issue.

WHO'S POINTING THE FINGER?

"Shirley, if you believe that God forgives you, then who is still pointing the finger of condemnation at you?"

"No one is! I am, plain and simple."

"Let me see, you do not feel condemned or judged by God, but you feel condemned by yourself?"

"You got it."

"You feel you need additional forgiveness above what God gives?"

"Well . . ."

I reached over the coffee table and handed her a Bible identical to mine. I then asked her to read Romans 8:31–39 aloud. She began reading slowly.

"'What then shall we say to these things? If God is for us, who is against us? He who did not spare His own Son, but delivered Him up for us all, how will He not also with Him freely give us all things.'"

She smiled with compliant agreement.

"Please read on."

"'Who will bring a charge against God's elect? God is the one who justifies.'"

"Who is the justifier?" I asked.

"God."

"Well, if God is the justifier, who else 'will bring a charge against God's elect?' Who else can point the finger at you, Shirley? Please read on."

She continued with hesitation in her voice, "'Who is the one who condemns?'"

"Go ahead! You can read it!" I prodded her. "Who is the one who would dare condemn?"

There was a silent pause.

"Why?" I asked.

"Because, 'Christ Jesus is He who died, yes, rather who was raised, who is at the right hand of God, who also intercedes for us.'"

"Shirley, does the 'who' in the first part of these verses include us?"

She reluctantly said, "Yes."

I continued: "I heard what you said, but I'm not sure you meant it from your heart. Do you understand that if you must forgive yourself you must also be able to justify yourself judiciously? That's impossible. Only God can justify. In order to forgive ourselves, we must first condemn ourselves, point the finger at ourselves, and this only results in false guilt."

FALSE GUILT

A glimmer of hope began to shine in Shirley's eyes. Why? Because faith to believe comes from hearing God's Word explained (Rom. 10:17). For Shirley, it was not just conflict between self-condemnation and God's justification, it was something deeper than that. It was false guilt. False guilt really makes forgiveness difficult. It muddies our minds and prompts us to feel the need to forgive ourselves in an attempt to get some badly needed relief.

Shirley clearly remembered the recent day that she genuinely repented and asked God to forgive her for her moral failures. But she did not feel forgiven. She felt she was still the object of condemnation, and thus needed to forgive herself.

"Shirley, do you know what guilt is?"

"Yes, it means that I deserve, or am worthy of, blame."

"Again, did you, in fact, ask God to forgive you for your moral failures?"

"Yes."

"Did He forgive you?"

"Yes."

"So, are you worthy of blame?"

"No . . . I mean yes . . . Well, I mean I know He forgave me, but that doesn't change the fact that I did those things."

"Yes, but 'If we confess our sins, he is faithful and just to forgive us our sins, and to cleanse us from all unrighteousness' (1 John 1:9 KJV). Did He forgive it all?"

"Yes."

"So are you still worthy of blame?"

She paused. Every emotion in her heart screamed yes, but then her mind took over and she said, "No, I guess not."

False guilt may not always be as simple to identify as this. For example, many women who have been molested as children feel they need to forgive themselves, but they can't because they feel partly responsible for the sexual abuse. They reason that there had to be something about them personally that caused the bad things to transpire in the first place. The logical conclusion is that they deserved the emotional and physical wounds they experienced. This often results in some women hating their own bodies, which they believe attracted the perpetrators to them. The result is a feeling of being bad, dirty, unforgivable, unlovable, unworthy, and certainly not deserving of honor (1 Pet. 3:7).

To add to the confusion, they may have experienced some pleasurable sensations during the sexual abuse. This is almost a guaranteed source of personal blame, shame, and self-condemnation. Sexual pleasure is a normal God-created function of the body, which can be involuntarily stimulated by another person in a situation that is beyond our control or consent. That sense of pleasure, even though stimulated involuntarily, feels good. Therefore, the victim of abuse reasons that she must be at fault because it felt good.

Unfortunately, adults can, and do, prematurely stimulate children sexually. If there is pleasure, this can lead the child to believe she liked it, or wanted it, and convince her that the perpetrators are just doing it because she liked it, or wanted it. Sex abuse counselors are very aware of this sexual brainwashing by perpetrators. However, no one would hold the child responsible for that premature activity, and neither does God. Even so, that child reaches adulthood confused and feeling guilty for a natural, though prematurely-activated, sexual sensation. These distorted perspectives wrongfully lead her, now as an adult, to feel a need to take God's forgiveness further, and forgive herself. Why? Because His forgiveness did not remove the continued self-condemning thoughts of false guilt and the deep sense of unworthiness.

POLYGRAPH TEST OF TRUTH

It is important to remember that, since false guilt and true guilt feel the same, both must be submitted to the true test of God's Word. I call it the "polygraph test of truth." Simply restated, when feeling guilty after confessing known sin to God, ask yourself, "Am I still worthy of blame even though I have been forgiven by God?" The answer is, "No, I'm not blameworthy." This must be accepted by faith in the facts of God's Word. The feelings will catch up later.

Some women feel that they are guilty for their molestation because they wanted to be near their father. The only time the father showed affection was at these times of sexual abuse. A major confusion sets in within the child. She begins to think that sex is love, and if you want love, you have to have sex. This is the reason many molested children are promiscuous in adolescence and even in adulthood.

This desire to be loved by their father is at the heart of most female promiscuity. I queried Shirley about her father. It did not take long to understand why she craved male attention. A critical, workaholic father, with sordid affairs sprinkled throughout his marriage, painted a painful backdrop against which Shirley acted out her immoral life. It was a life rooted in bitterness, not pleasure.

Most men wrongfully think an immoral woman is driven by her lust. Wrong! It is all too often an inner craving to be loved or comforted by her father. A woman will trade sex for "love," and a man will give "love" for sex. Often, her motivation is rooted in bitterness toward men, and not in a love for men. True guilt for adult immorality gets confused with false childhood guilt and becomes a perfect setup for a no-win situation. No distinction is made between the separate guilt issues, and they are not dealt with separately and biblically. As a result, the person feels the need to forgive themselves, and true resolution of the guilt never takes place. However, when they clearly understand the distinction between what was done to them as children, and what they are feeling in adulthood, many are relieved. They stop assuming childhood responsibility that is not theirs and start claiming responsibility for the adult behavior which is theirs.

Then the big question arises, "What if I initiated the sexual contact with my dad as a child?" You may have done that, it is true. But the real issue is: Who set you up for it as a child? Jesus clarified who had the primary responsibility in these situations. He acknowledged that stumbling blocks will be set up by others that will either impede growth or stop it all together. But He then concluded that for those who cause this stumbling, "It would be better for him if a millstone were hung around his neck and he were thrown into the sea" (Luke 17:1–2).

A distorted perspective and misbelief can very easily prevent one from placing responsibility where it belongs, and then granting genuine forgiveness to the offender and purposing to live in the freedom of release. False guilt, if not seen for what it is, can become the seed bed for a misperceived need of self-forgiveness.

SORROW AND REGRET

Another major confusion that can lead someone to feel the need to forgive himself has to do with the concept of regret. This struck a familiar chord in Shirley's heart.

Men recall relational events in general terms—short on details. Women, however, remember both in detail and Technicolor. This balance can be an asset to a couple if they understand and appreciate the difference. If they don't, however, it can be the basis for a holy war and painful conflict.

Shirley's memory vividly recalled her moral failures. She understood intellectually that God had forgiven her, but her regret brought confusion to the issue of forgiveness. Guilt and regret are two different issues and should not be confused. True guilt is like a built-in alarm system to notify us of the presence of a sin. Once we have confessed our sin, it is forgiven, and genuine guilt should cease. But, as I have said, false guilt can seep in and produce guilt feelings. Remember, false and true guilt feel the same. For that reason they must be tested with truth.

I began to see that Shirley was not just feeling guilt but regret, which is a form of sadness. Sadness is a normal emotion. It is not the same as depression, although it can lead to depression if it is sustained over the course of time. Shirley was feeling a sense of regret and normal sadness over her moral choices. I explained to her that sadness and remorse are normal emotions in the grief process of any loss. Healthy grief begins by admitting that a loss has occurred. This is an important step in overcoming denial. Next, there is the emotional response of anger. Then there is bargaining with God, or "magical thinking," that wishes the loss had not occurred, or that someone could have done something to prevent it. Normally, sadness soon follows, and, finally, there is acceptance of the loss.

Shirley had lost her innocence, but she was forgiven by God. God does not condemn her at all (Rom. 8:1). Shirley, however, was condemning herself because she felt the normal feelings of sadness and regret. It is a good sign of mental health to be able to process loss and go through all of its stages. But when Shirley got stuck in regret (the bargaining or "if only" cycle of the grief process), she responded by confusing normal grieving with her perceived need to forgive herself. Because of this, she was not able to focus on processing the loss.

Sorrow can be from God, and if it is, it leads to repentance. If repentance is completed, the remaining sadness is not a moral issue, but a normal sorrow from experiencing loss. By contrast, sorrow produced by the world system leads to death or thoughts of suicide. But sorrow from God will lead to repentance (change of direction and behavior) and salvation (2 Cor. 7:10).

FALSE REPENTANCE

Three words often get confused with repentance: sorrow, regret, and remorse. Repentance means making a 180-degree

U-turn (change) in behavior by going in the opposite direction. Let's suppose we are standing in the center of a huge clock. Facing straight ahead of us is the 12 o'clock position. Directly behind us is the 6 o'clock position. Sorrow is mental suffering caused by a loss or sin. I can feel sorry that I did something and make a small directional change in my behavior. That is, I can go from the 12 o'clock position to the 1 o'clock position. I am sorry, and I make a slight behavioral change. This is not repentance.

A deeper sorrow can lead to regret. I regret what I did so I make a behavioral change, and now I'm facing the 3 o'clock position. I have now gone from 12 o'clock to 3 o'clock—a 90-degree or right-angle change in behavior. But a right angle turn is not a U-turn. It is not repentance.

Then, a deep regret can lead to remorse. We are getting close now. But remorse is only at the 5 o'clock position. At least I am getting close to the 6 o'clock (U-turn) position. Look how much I've changed. Yes, remorse is close, but it is not repentance. Repentance is a complete U-turn from 12 o'clock to 6 o'clock. It means an absolute change and a brokenness of our core belief system, called the heart (Ps. 51:16). Repentance takes sorrow, regret, and remorse, and translates them into a 180-degree change in direction, not a mere course deviation.

When the apostle Paul spoke in his own defense before King Agrippa, he explained what repentance included: ". . . that they [the Gentiles] should repent and turn to God, performing deeds appropriate to repentance" (Acts 26:20). Likewise, he described the conversion and repentance of the Thessalonians by describing how they "turned to God from idols to serve a living and true God" (1 Thess. 1:9). That is, they made a complete U-turn in their behavior and in their lifestyle.

People have wept buckets of tears in my office as a result of deep sorrow, regret, and even remorse. Now emotionally relieved, they feel lighter. But sadly, they only make partial changes in their behavior and think it is a total directional change. Yes, they experienced deep emotional release, but that is not repentance. Shirley was a classic example. After each crisis pregnancy, she expressed deep regret but turned around and did the very same thing over again. The core issues, namely, forgiveness of her father and acceptance of forgiveness by her Heavenly Father, were not completely addressed and changed. Therefore, the behavior was only temporarily modified.

Again, true repentance is an absolute about-face. Unfortunately, this is so rare that we have grown to believe that even a partial change of behavior (resulting from sorrow, regret, and remorse) is, in fact, repentance. But this false, shallow, incomplete repentance leaves one with a nagging guilt. Having wrongly concluded that one has really repented, the feelings of the residual guilt lead one to the conclusion he must do something else, i.e., forgive himself. Again, instead of reexamining his heart and evaluating whether or not true repentance has actually taken place, energies are diverted to vain attempts at self-forgiveness.

How seriously did Jesus view repentance? Very seriously! Listen to this: "I tell you...unless you repent, you will all likewise perish" (Luke 13:5). Godly sorrow over emotional pain results in genuine repentance. Peter experienced this. He denied his association with Jesus three times. After the cock crowed, Peter was devastated by guilt as Jesus' prediction of denial came to pass. Peter was overwhelmed by guilt and sorrow, and responded with repentance, and by weeping bitterly (Luke 22:62). He then returned to serve the Lord. He did what Jesus foretold to Peter: "When once you have turned again, strengthen your brothers" (Luke 22:32). Judas, on the contrary, who betrayed the Lord, acknowledged he had sinned by betraying innocent blood and felt remorse. However, rather than turning back to God, he hung himself (Matt. 27:3–5).

This time Shirley was genuinely broken. Yes, there were tears as there were before. But this time I could tell they were tears of true repentance, and I was able to witness the U-turn. Once Shirley understood that her godly sorrow was designed to lead her to biblical repentance and forgiveness, and that the residual regret or sadness was normal, a great look of relief spread across her face. I then reminded her again that she needed to allow the past forgiven memory to be a springboard to praise and an appreciation for God's grace (1 Cor. 15:10).

MENTAL LIBRARY

Feelings usually respond to thoughts. As Shirley would reflect on her losses, the emotions of sadness and regret followed. Feelings respond as readily to truth as they do to the lies or misconceptions that we hold in life. This is what made it hard for Shirley to fully accept God's forgiveness as the complete provision for her moral failure. She held many false beliefs at the core of her thinking. Solomon described the relationship between thinking and acting in this way: "For as he thinks within himself, so he is" (Prov. 23:7). In other words, whatever a person believes about himself (or God) in the core of his heart, that is what is reality to him, and this is the reality he will act upon.

I drew a word picture to help Shirley visualize the concept

of core beliefs. I asked her to picture her mind like a large university library; each core belief was like a book.

Volume 1: "I Am Unworthy"

Let's suppose you were assigned a research paper on worthiness. You go to the library and peruse the stacks under the heading of "worth." You pull a volume off the shelf and read, "I am an unworthy person." You did not put the volume in the library—someone else did. But this is the only book on the subject, so it must be true. Therefore, the thesis of my paper will be, "I am an unworthy person."

Perhaps the most frequent lie I hear in this regard is this: "I am unworthy to be forgiven; therefore, I can't forgive myself." Here the confusion is between the issues of worthiness and forgiveness. First, it is very important to realize that none of us are worthy in and of ourselves. True, we are created in the image of God and we are loved by God (Gen. 1:26; John 3:16). But we have all sinned (Rom. 3:23), and the penalty for that sin is death (Rom. 6:23). This is true even though we are deeply loved by God (Rom. 5:8). We were not saved out of human effort on our behalf, but by His grace and mercy (Eph. 2:8–9). We are fully accepted in Christ (Rom. 15:7), because our worthiness is in Christ.

The person struggling with worthiness may have had a difficult past which unintentionally placed the volume of "unworthiness" in his mental library. Not only do these painful elements skew our perception of ourselves, they also color our perception of God and His Word. As a result, a misbelief regarding our own worth in Christ develops. And, if we do not think we are worthy in Christ, we will logically reject His forgiveness and resort to forgiving ourselves to get relief.

Volume 2: "I Am to Blame"

Perhaps the second most frequent lie to be pulled from the library of our mind is: "It's all my fault. I am to blame." This usually reflects a myopic childlike perspective of life, which is carried into adulthood. If I was raised in a malfunctioning home where I was blamed for everything, I will keep that myopic outlook in adulthood and continue to believe the lie that I am responsible and blameworthy for everything. Now, as an adult, I know better. But the continued childlike perspective sucks me into a vicious cycle: "I am responsible; therefore, I need to forgive myself. But I can't, because I am not worthy to be forgiven, since it is all my fault."

Self-blame is the perfect setup for feeling the need to forgive yourself. The solution for this misconception is still rooted in the seed of "renewing your mind" (Rom. 12:2), or changing the way you think. You must put away the childlike myopic view of life that believes you are to blame for everything (1 Cor. 13:11). You must accept the fact that others too have responsibility, that the world does not revolve around you, and that you are never totally to blame for everything. True, you are responsible for your own actions and attitudes, but not the actions of the whole world. The things we are legitimately responsible for we should confess, repent, and then bask in the pure delight of God's forgiveness (1 John 1:9).

Volume 3: "I Am Not Lovable"

This leads us to another conflict that feeds the need to forgive ourselves. Often our greatest hurts are those caused by our parents. One of the biggest reasons we are unable to assign appropriate responsibility to our parents for their failures is this: If we fully acknowledge their offenses, we will falsely conclude that "they do not love me" and therefore "I am unlovable." Most of us can't stand that feeling. Most every parent offends their children in some way, yet still deeply loves them. As a parent and grandparent I can personally attest to that. But that childlike, false belief cannot understand this, even though, in reality, it happens every day.

The lie that we are not lovable and that no one could love us sets the stage for not feeling loved by God. Thus we feel that we are not forgiven—or even forgivable—by God. The net result is this: If God doesn't love me, He won't forgive me. Therefore, I must forgive myself.

The lie that I am not lovable is one hundred percent contrary to God's Word! We were created to be loved. God deeply loves us in spite of our sins (Rom. 5:8). We must therefore, by faith, release that childhood lie ("Volume 3" from the mental library) and replace it with the truth: I am unconditionally loved and fully accept God's forgiveness. This is a much better plan than trying to practice self-forgiveness, which only tends to skirt the real core issues and even, on occasion, perpetrates false feelings of self-hatred.

Volume 4: "I Hate Myself"

Self-hate is usually not only one volume—but a whole set of encyclopedias. There are at least three sources of self-hatred. First, is a misplaced hate toward someone else. A person may have a strong anger toward a parent that he feels unable to acknowledge, so he turns it on himself. This is like pointing a gun toward the parent, but the barrel is actually bent back on himself, so, when he pulls the trigger, it explodes on himself instead.

It almost seems like an axiom of life that those who hate

their parents seem to hate themselves. The reason is simple. If we derive our sense of who we are from our parents as children, then how we view them will contribute to how we see ourselves. The opposite also seems to be true. If we have an appropriate love for our parents, it seems to result in our feeling better about ourselves (Eph. 6:2–3). However, when the object of anger is our parents, we tend to turn the anger in on ourselves, and this often leads to depression.

The second source of self-hatred is the misbelief that I have done something so bad that God cannot forgive me. I hate myself for it, and feel God can't forgive me. So, I'm stuck having to forgive myself. The solution is not to forgive yourself, but to learn a more biblical view of God. I believe A.W. Tozer reflected this when he said that "our problems, and their solutions, are theological" (*The Knowledge of the Holy*, p. 27). Why would this be true in this instance? Because the problem is in our misunderstanding of God's grace and mercy. Grace is God granting us favor we do not deserve. Mercy is God withholding something negative (i.e., judgment) that we do deserve. We deserve wrath, but it is withheld, because it has already been directed at Christ on the cross.

The third source of self-hatred can come from our response to tragedies. Job experienced this. After he lost his sheep, camels, oxen, donkeys, servants, all his children, and finally his health, his wife counseled him to curse God (take revenge) and die (escape) (Job 2:9). Job could not bring his righteous heart to curse God. But he did do something else—he cursed himself. He cursed the day he was born and all the events surrounding it (Job 3:1–20). This is a great illustration of anger turned inward. The logic is simple. If I had not been born, I would not have experienced these losses and ensuing pain. This thinking usually reflects a misbelief that life should be pain free. The active pursuit of this goal of a pain free life can serve as a doorway to a mental breakdown. The deep regret or hatred for being born only feeds shame, cuts us off from God, and leaves us still needing the relief of forgiveness. Conclusion? God is factored out. I'm the only one left—I guess I just need to forgive myself. No! Factor God back in and work through the serious losses biblically.

THE ROOTS OF SELF-FORGIVENESS

A Historical Development

The concept of self-forgiveness is not new. Almost all psychological theories recognize the need to exercise some form of forgiveness or release. Different words or procedures may be utilized, but they all have some form of release involved. Because many of the secular personality theories were designed by people who did not believe in a higher power—let alone a personal God—they were caught in a dilemma. The tool of release is valid, but if I do not believe in a personal God, to whom, or to what can I turn to gain forgiveness? Bingo! Me! Why ask a God I don't believe in to forgive me when I can just ask and receive forgiveness from myself. This practice of self-forgiveness unintentionally tends to deify the self as the ultimate granter of forgiveness. This practice of self-forgiveness has seeped into Christian writings and preaching and is now preached and taught as if it is a normal Bible-taught pattern to follow in the Christian life.

As stated earlier, the concept of self-forgiveness is not taught or illustrated in Scripture. I would encourage you to address the other issues first, before quickly resorting to self-forgiveness. Addressing these other issues may actually be the key to freedom for you, a freedom which relieves you of the need you feel to forgive yourself.

Self-Love

Another root of self-forgiveness is found in the concept of self-love. Those who counsel that we are to forgive ourselves use for support the passage that declares, "You shall love your neighbor as yourself" (Matt. 19:19). They reason that, if you really love yourself, you will forgive yourself. By self-love, they do not mean a total absorption by the self (as experienced in narcissism), or a total self-glorification, or a haughty arrogance that looks down on others. Rather, their focus is primarily on the worth and dignity of man, which is based on being created in the image of God. But two theological extremes rarely get blended into a healthy balance—depravity and dignity. Both are taught in Scripture. Human dignity is rooted in the basis of our being created in the image of God (Gen. 1:27). We have innate worth (Matt. 6:26). However, we are also born into sin (Rom. 3:10–18).

The logic of forgiving ourselves based on self-love runs along these lines. The Bible commands us to love our neighbor as we do ourselves. Since we are obligated to forgive our neighbor out of love for him, should we not likewise forgive ourselves out of our love for ourselves? It may be helpful here to clarify a few crucial issues. First, Matthew 19:19 does not command us to love ourselves. The word "as" (*hos*, in the Greek) is a word comparison, not a command. True, self-love is assumed in this and other passages. For example, husbands are to love their wives as their own bodies. By doing so, they love themselves because no one ever "hated his own flesh, but nourishes and cherishes it" (Eph. 5:28–29). However, the command here (in Matt. 19:19) is not to love ourselves, but to love others (your "neighbor").

Nowhere in Scripture do we see self-love as a basis for obedience to God. The apostle Paul had kept his body under control morally to keep from being "disqualified" (literally, "unapproved"). He was concerned that his ministry could be cut short through the disciplinary disapproval of God (1 Cor. 9:27). But he also anticipated fighting a good fight, finishing the course, and keeping the faith. Why? Because he longingly anticipated receiving the crown of righteousness that will be awarded by the Lord personally to Paul and to all who have loved His appearing (2 Tim. 4:7–8). But Jesus said it best when He said: "If you love Me [not "yourself"], you will keep My commandments" (John 14:15). Our love for God is in response to His love for us: "In this is love, not that we loved God, but that He loved us and sent His Son to be the propitiation for our sins" (1 John 4:10). Self-love never figures into the obedience equation.

Absence of a Pattern

Furthermore, never in all my reading of Scripture have I found an illustration, a pattern to follow, or a direct injunction to forgive ourselves. Every time I have tried to think about how I would counsel someone to do it or lead them in prayer to do it, I have come up blank. I have tried writing out a prayer that accomplishes this: "Dear God, I now forgive myself for hurting my Christian brother. I know You have forgiven me, but I now forgive myself." One might say, "What's wrong with that?" Simple. The "you" you forgive is the same person who did the offense. "I forgive me." You would have to be a split personality to actually do this. It reinforces disassociative behavior. James describes a person who habitually doubts as a "double-minded man" (*dipsuchos*, in the Greek), a man who is unstable in all his ways (James 1:8). But the double-minded person is not two people, he's one individual who wavers first one way, and then another. He is not a split personality.

We are clearly instructed to confess our sins (1 John 1:9; James 5:16). When we do, "He [God] is faithful and just to forgive us our sins, and to cleanse us from all unrighteousness" (1 John 1:9 KJV). If we are cleansed, what else is there to do to receive forgiveness? Is forgiveness in stages, first God, then us? No. God's forgiveness is complete. We do not need to forgive ourselves.

Biblical Word

Finally, I believe the root meaning of the New Testament word for "forgive" (*aphiemi*) may ultimately clarify the issue. Aphiemi, "forgive," primarily means "to send forth" (*apo*, "from"; *hiemi*, "to send"). It denotes a complete removal of the cause of the offense. This remission is based on the substitutionary sacrifice of Christ (2 Cor. 5:21). He took our sins away from us and put them on Himself. Therefore God emphatically declares: "Who will bring a charge against God's elect?" (Rom. 8:33). This seals the issue: No one can, not even ourselves!

FREEDOM AT LAST

Jesus defined the basis for our freedom. It rests in abiding in His Word (living a lifestyle that reflects what He has established in His spoken Word) and in His personal example. His living Word, clearly lived out in practice, will result in freedom (John 8:31–32).

This is where Shirley ultimately found freedom. Once all the other confusing issues and opinions of men were replaced with a biblically based belief system, she was free to walk down the path of true forgiveness, and be the morally responsible person God intended her to be.

◊

There is yet another hindrance to realizing forgiveness fully. It is based on a confusing "truth" that is widely preached and taught, but does not reflect clear theology. Carol had to wrestle with this one before she was able to come to peace after a major loss.

Chapter 9

"I Can't Forgive God!"

God is a joke," Carol blurted out. "If He can't even watch over my only son, what business does He have running a universe? If I had ten kids, yes, it would be hard to lose one, but my only son? My husband was unfaithful all of our twenty-three years of marriage. And, do you know how many cancer surgeries I've had to go through just to be here today? I know I shouldn't feel this way. Yes, I'm a Christian, but I'm a bitter one."

Angry at God. This is not new. Scripture bears record of many individuals and nations that were angry at God. Even godly men were angry at God at times. When King David was returning the ark of God from the hill country to the City of David, a tragedy occurred. Instead of being carried by two poles through the rings on each side, the ark of God was being transported on a cart. Uzzah, reaching out to steady the ark when the oxen had nearly upset it, was struck dead by God. "And David became angry because of the Lord's outburst against Uzzah" (2 Sam. 6:8). Although David's intentions to relocate the ark to Jerusalem were pure, he had unintentionally violated God's clear procedure for transporting the ark of God (Exod. 25:10–15).

As we discussed in chapter two, anger is an automatic emotional response to a perceived or actual offense. David perceived that God overreacted by killing Uzzah. What David failed to see initially was that, to touch the ark of God was an act of irreverence and a direct violation of God's absolute holiness. His holiness demanded that sacred tasks be carried out in a sacred manner. Someone could have counseled David to forgive God. But was David's need to forgive God or to understand the character of God? True, the normal biblical tool to deal with an offense resulting in anger is forgiveness. But what if this anger is directed toward God?

Today, many pastors, teachers, and Christian psychologists and psychiatrists take anger a step further and suggest that the offended one should even forgive God. I was listening intently to a Christian psychiatrist deliver an excellent message on scriptural forgiveness and the importance of it from a mental health perspective. He declared that, in addition to forgiving others, you will need to forgive yourself. Then, without a pause, he said, "You may even need to forgive God." In lowered tones he conceded, however, ". . . really, God does not need to be forgiven, but you may have to do it anyway." It is this kind of spiritual counseling double-talk that confuses many sincere believers who already find it hard to work through their personal struggle with forgiveness.

What we are going to discover in this chapter is that the issue here as it relates to God is not forgiveness, but trust, acceptance, and, if possible, understanding. Why is this distinction important? Because if we divert our attention and energies to the misguided need to forgive God, we will never return to the more crucial issues of trust and acceptance. Without the latter two, anger will continue into bitterness, and genuine closure, resulting in trust and acceptance, will not be achieved.

There are at least three problems with the perceived need to forgive God: it implies 1) an offense, 2) accountability, and 3) payment. We will look at each of these.

FORGIVENESS IMPLIES AN OFFENSE

Before one can legitimately use the biblical tool of forgiveness, there has to be an identifiable offense on someone's part. On the human level, it is possible to offend someone either intentionally or unintentionally, out of commission or omission.

I have done my share of asking forgiveness for things that I intentionally did out of my own selfishness or fleshly behavior. God's faithful conviction reminded me of my sin. I have offended family, friends, coworkers, parishioners—to say nothing of those I have offended in the service industries with my impatience, lack of understanding, or ignorance. To make matters worse, at times I have offended all the above unintentionally and unknowingly. Sometimes I did so by things I sincerely thought were right at the time, but later came to realize were wrong. At other times I was just plain insensitive. Yes, "to err is human," but I must still confess my sin to those I offended and prayerfully hope for their forgiveness.

On the other hand, there were times I had to make a decision as a college administrator that did not set well with particular staff or students. After painstaking evaluation, prayer, and counsel, the decision was made. It was my responsibility to do so. I had not sinned, but my action did offend. In this case, the need of the staff and students was not forgiveness of the administrator, but acceptance of the decision or policy. This did not mean they could not submit an appeal. A wise leader must possess a willingness to be reasonable (James 3:17), and allow for this possibility.

Sometimes, too, church leadership may have to make a decision for the church body that is not liked by all, but is the morally right decision. A morally right decision can still offend. But again, the need here is not forgiveness, but trust, acceptance, and understanding.

It is important to note that, when we look at God's dealing with man, God does not—nor can He ever—sin against us either intentionally or unintentionally (James 1:13). There is no sin in Him (Heb. 4:15). All of us at one time or another have had the same problem with God as the college staff and students had with me, or church members may have with their leadership. Or, for that matter, children have with their parents. We, as humans, can sincerely mean well and still make wrong decisions. But God never makes a wrong decision or morally offends us. Therefore, God never needs to be forgiven. Instead, we need to learn to trust Him and come to closure through acceptance. Yes, we can become offended at God because we do not like His decision. But this is not a moral offense that needs to be forgiven—it's a moral decision that needs to be accepted.

Yet from Carol's perspective, God does not get off that easy. When she received a call from the city police that her son was in the hospital with serious injuries, her emotions broke loose. Her whole life and reason for living was now threatened and would soon come crashing down. Carol's major complaint about God was one I have heard many times before. In fact, it is probably the number one alleged offense by God—He failed to protect. And to make matters worse, in Carol's case, it was her only son.

Carol sincerely believed in her heart that a good God does not let bad things happen to His people. Bad things only happen to bad people. This is the same erroneous perspective the disciples held when they asked Jesus to clarify the origin of a man's blindness from birth: "Rabbi, who sinned, this man or his parents, that he should be born blind?" Jesus expanded their thinking when He answered, "It was neither that this man sinned, nor his parents; but it was in order that the works of God might be displayed in him" (John 9:2–3). When a circumstance in our life does not turn out according to our understanding of the character of God, we translate that into an offense by God. If God does not "perform" as I believe He should, He has offended me. However, the real failure is not with God's performance; it is with our misperception, or imperfect knowledge of the most Holy.

Take the apostle Paul, for example. If bad things only happened to bad people, then Paul could be rated as the worst person who ever lived! Scripture tells us that he was faced with frequent beatings, imprisonments, stonings, and shipwrecks—among other calamities (2 Cor. 11:22–33). But his personal losses did not reflect a lack of moral character. No, we would not even suggest that. Rather, Paul understood he was called to suffer loss, and through it learn what it meant to experience the fellowship of the Lord Jesus' sufferings (Phil. 3:10; Acts 9:16).

As Carol shared her anger and rage, I knew better than to try to explain anything then. There is a time to listen and a time to talk (Eccles. 3:7; James 1:19). Later, however, I asked her to explain what she was taught about God and

His protective care, and what role suffering played in the Christian experience. Saner moments brought Carol back to her good biblical training, but the shock, loss, and grief threw her into a crisis that caused all of her normal coping mechanisms to fail.

But Carol is not alone. Adults who were abused as children also struggle with this perceived lack of God's protection. Where was God when this happened, and why didn't He stop it? This is a very difficult issue to understand fully, even for the best of us. Did He know it was going to happen? Yes, He is omniscient. Was He there when it happened? Yes, He is omnipresent. Did He have enough power to stop it? Yes, He is omnipotent. Then why didn't He do something to stop it? Doesn't He love us?

Contrary to all the recorded history of God's goodness to man, we still judge Him primarily on the basis of what He has done or failed to do for us personally. The crucial issue here is a failure to understand that God does not normally suspend the consequential laws of sin for believers. One out of every four women have been sexually abused as children. In boys, it's one out of six. Pedophiles perpetrate their sin on innocent children. Drunk drivers carelessly careen into oncoming traffic and kill thousands of innocent people. But if a person does not understand and accept the reality of sin and its consequences, he can become bitter at God and wrongly conclude that he must somehow forgive God for His failure to intervene. Remember, however, the crucial issue here is trust, not forgiveness. God is more angry at perpetrators or abusers than we could ever be. "If this is true," you may ask, "why doesn't He just zap these wicked people?" Good question. Peter answered it: "The Lord is not slow about His promise [of judgment and destruction of ungodly men], as some count slowness, but is patient toward you, not wishing for any to perish but for all to come to repentance." Then he concludes, "But the day of the Lord will come like a thief, in which the heavens will pass away with a roar and the elements will be destroyed with intense heat, and the earth and its works will be burned up" (2 Pet. 3:9–10). The holy terror and destruction of the great tribulation and subsequent judgments does not make sense apart from understanding the anger God has for all the wickedness in the world. He is graciously patient now, but will be equally wrathful later.

In addition to a perceived lack of protection by God, acts of nature such as earthquakes, tornadoes, hurricanes, floods, fires, droughts, as well as birth defects and diseases are also perceived as offenses by God against man. This was true in Carol's case as well. Not only had she lost her only son, she had bravely fought cancer for years. Her prognosis went from month to month. Accepting the cancer was hard enough.

TRIAL EXEMPT

Many people assume that God is under contract to make their life free of pain and loss, especially if they are faithful in their relationship with Him. We as a church may be tax exempt, but we are not trial exempt. Related to this are the people who are bitter at God because someone they know and love walked consistently with God and was tragically killed or suffered a prolonged, excruciating illness. They fail to remember two very important things: First, God does not suspend the natural laws of nature for believers. Believers develop cancer and die. I have personally grieved the loss of godly friends who have succumbed to the ravages of cancer.

But the opposite is also true. The Lord Jesus, in giving a glimpse of the character of God, said, "Love your enemies, and pray for those who persecute you in order that you may be sons of your Father who is in heaven." He then shares an important insight on the character of God: "For He causes His sun to rise on the evil and the good, and sends rain on the righteous and the unrighteous" (Matt. 5:44–45). Just as natural benefits fall both to the just and the unjust, so the results of natural disasters fall on both the godly and the ungodly. When God suspends a natural law, we call it a "miracle." Miracles do happen from time to time, but they are not normative. Secondly, while we have the promise that all pain and tears will be wiped away in heaven, this is earth. Jesus clearly demonstrated this understanding as He faced the agonies of death on the Cross: "Who for the joy set before Him [in heaven] endured the cross [on earth]" (Heb. 12:2).

Another perceived offense by God against man comes in the form of economic reversals (personal or business related). I have counseled many who have lost everything financially and were bitter at God. Family reversals, death, divorce, affairs, rebellious children, prodigal spouses, parental abandonment, church fights, and disillusionment in Christian service all contribute to anger and bitterness toward God. Books roll off the presses by good authors trying to explain or make sense out of what God is doing in the midst of their disappointment with Him. Many of these are helpful. However, many of these fail to help a believer distinguish between forgiving God and trusting God by accepting adversity from Him.

The most godly of men in Scripture have had to struggle with economic reversals or the loss of material things. Job is a classic example. After Job's wife counseled Job to "curse God and die," Job asked her a probing question: "Shall we indeed accept good from God and not accept adversity?" (Job 2:9–10). Like Job's wife, we are not usually willing to allow for the option of adversity. But it is important to know one thing here. Most Bible scholars believe that Job was the first book written in the Bible, and, if this is true, the problem of pain and human suffering was the first problem God addressed in His Word! Adversity in this world is a given, whether you are a believer or not.

It is interesting to note that James is believed to be the first book written in the New Testament. And what is the first issue God addresses in James? Loss from trials! The letter is addressed to the twelve tribes (of Israel) who are dispersed abroad. They were being "surrounded" (Greek, *peripesete*) by trials, and James attempts to adjust their attitude to see these trials not as tribulations but as tests designed to build the godly character of patience. Trials, from this perspective, are to be welcomed—not resented. They are to be responded to with joy, not because we escape them, but because we know God's purpose for them—the godly quality of endurance. God knew that hurt and loss would come to His children, but He wanted to turn it into a benefit for them.

FORGIVENESS IMPLIES ACCOUNTABILITY

The second thing forgiveness implies is accountability. One of the questions we most frequently ask God is "Why?" "Why did I lose the farm? Why did my wife die leaving three small children? Why were five Christian coeds hit head-on by a drunk driver?" A "why" question was even once directed to God the Father by Jesus Himself. While in physical and emotional agony on the cross he cried out: "My God, My God, why hast Thou forsaken Me?" (Matt. 27:46).

It is important to understand here that it is one thing to ask why; it is yet another to demand that God answer it to our satisfaction. "Why" questions imply accountability. The offender is accountable to the one offended to acknowledge the wrong. From there he may also be held accountable to explain why he did it, and even perhaps, why he did not make restitution when it was in his power to do so. It requires the offender to humble himself and acknowledge his wrong.

It is a humbling experience to admit one's error and ask forgiveness. However, if God is to be forgiven, must He humble Himself and ask our forgiveness? Are we going to cut off fellowship with Him until He does? Many have. As we pointed out in chapter 6, fellowship is impeded if acknowledgment of a wrong is not forthcoming. Must God acknowledge He was wrong or explain His actions before we can continue a relationship (fellowship) with Him? Forgiving God would have to include God humbling Himself and acknowledging His wrong before the relationship could be restored, thus making Him accountable to us. When viewed like this, the whole concept of forgiving God is absurd. Yet, it is perpetuated as a means of attaining sound mental health by pastors and Christian mental health workers alike. When it is not thought through to its logical conclusion, however, much energy is diverted to the vain attempt to forgive God and not properly channeled to acceptance and trust in God.

This whole concept of accountability also seems to have reversed the roles of God and man. Paul makes it clear who should be asking what of whom when he declared, "Who are you, O man, who answers back to God? The thing molded [man] will not say to the molder [God], 'Why did you make me like this,' will it? Or does not the potter have a right over the clay, to make from the same lump one vessel for honorable use, and another for common use?" (Rom. 9:20–21). Jesus, too, illustrated the proper way to question God and accept His will at the same time: "If it is possible, let this cup pass from Me; yet not as I will, but as Thou wilt" (Matt. 26:39). And just in case one may be inclined to think this was not a struggle for the Son of God, remember, He asked His Father three times in similar words to be released but concluded each request in the same fashion: ". . . yet not My will but Thine be done." To expect God to bow down to man in such a way is irreverent, to say the least. The fact is, Jesus has already humbled Himself to the lowest point possible—the point of death—and He did so to purchase our salvation because we have offended Him—not He us! (Phil. 2:5–11) He is now exalted in Heaven where He will remain until His return (1 Thess. 4:13–18). Praise God!

FORGIVENESS IMPLIES PAYMENT

Finally, forgiveness implies the necessity of a payment. As we discussed in chapter 4, someone has to pay for our sin and offenses before they can be forgiven. However, if God has offended us, for whatever perceived reason, who is going to pay for that offense? There was only one perfect sacrifice for sin (2 Cor. 5:21). There is only one true God who can offer that sacrifice. It took the death of Christ, the God-Man, to pay for all sin. Who then is going to die to pay for His offense?

The absurdity of forgiving God only increases when we analyze the biblical concept of forgiveness. There is no scriptural record of God acknowledging the need to be forgiven by anyone.

ACCEPTANCE AND TRUST

Why didn't I defend God to Carol while she was releasing her anger toward God and others for her son's death? Simple. She was angry, her emotions were ruling, and her reasoning was not prevailing at the time. However, the more she was allowed to ask the questions and express her feelings, the more I could see God beginning to gently comfort her. Frankly, she was stuck in the second phase of grief. The actual steps of grief have been debated, but as we have mentioned before, they usually include these five elements: denial, anger, bargaining ("if onlys"), sadness, and finally, acceptance. Most who have been bitter for some time are stuck in the second phase of grief, namely, anger.

Some may suggest that you need to forgive God in order to get out of the anger stage. True, there is a place for forgiveness of sin in the anger stage, and it is appropriate to exercise it against legitimate offenders. However, I strongly question using an unbiblical procedure to get a highly emotional, partially irrational person through the anger stage of grief. Anger is very blame-oriented. Anger and blame are bedfellows. Our natural instinct in a crisis is to quickly attack and cast blame in order to create an outlet for our anger. But true guilt means the offender is worthy of blame. Is God worthy of blame? This issue is key if you are to process your anger through forgiveness to acceptance. You must acknowledge the hurt and anger, yes. But at the same time you must recognize that what you need more than forgiving God is to accept the loss and trust Him in it.

I was speaking at a rustic family camp in Wisconsin one summer. During one of the afternoon breaks, my family and I were enjoying some of the lakefront activities when a

middle-aged conferee introduced herself to me. Verna startled me with her next statement: "I hate Romans 8:28!"
Trying to appear calm, I said, "Oh?" masking my shock. I
spent the next two hours listening to the details of the horrific accident which resulted in her husband's death and multiple surgeries for her.

According to her story, the gracious outpouring of many
Christian friends was amazing. However, person after person made reference to Romans 8:28 on their sympathy
card: ". . . and we know that all things work together for
good . . ." (KJV). Despite their sincere efforts to comfort
and console her, her emotions still screamed within her: "I
will not accept his death, and I refuse to believe that all
this pain is going to benefit anyone!" She was in the full-
blown second phase of grieving—anger.

Our family developed a friendship with Verna over the
years. Yes, she did move through the grieving stages from
"God owes me an apology" to "It hurts, but now I can accept
the accident and live in peace with the losses." Did God need
to be forgiven? No. Did Verna grow in her trust and acceptance? Yes.

Most people are able to move through the anger phase
more easily if someone will take the time to grant some non-
judgmental understanding, then gently lead them to the more
crucial issue of acceptance. Acceptance is not a matter of
understanding (which is a function of the mind), but of trust
(which is a function of our will through faith) (Heb. 11:6).

I often hear people say that they cannot wait to get to
heaven and ask God why He did what He did. I am quite
confident that God is not anxiously awaiting our arrival and
the subsequent grilling He is going to receive. I believe our
knowledge and understanding will be instantly expanded,

and the need to make a sovereign God give us an account of His actions will instantly dissipate. Paul expressed it this way: "For now we see in a mirror dimly, but then face to face; now I know in part, but then I shall know fully just as I also have been fully known" (1 Cor. 13:12).

Corrie ten Boom used to give a good illustration of this in her talks. She would show the backside of a tapestry with all its tangled and knotted strands of yarn at varying lengths. It looked like a mess from the underside, but then she would turn it over so we could see the beautiful design. Our questions disappeared when we saw the intricate pattern so carefully designed. This, I believe, is how it will be when we are transported from here to glory. Down here on earth, we are looking at the underside of this tapestry called life. When we get to heaven, however, we will get to see the beautiful design on the other side, and all our doubts and perplexities will vanish.

PAIN AND ACCEPTANCE

Acceptance was not easy for Carol. She had sustained a lot of losses in life, the greatest of which was the loss of her son. Did she ever come to the place of releasing all the pain and never feeling that loss again? No. Acceptance does not mean the pain is totally gone. Much of the tragic pain we experience in life will subside, but not fully vanish this side of heaven. Will she always have a sense of loss and some residual pain? Yes. Some would say that if she fully accepted the loss of her son, she would no longer feel the pain of it. Unfortunately, these sincere people confuse acceptance with absence of pain. In reality, pain may or may not be there. If it is, it can be in varying degrees. But quiet acceptance does not mean she will have no continued sense of loss when she attends a wedding, sees someone else with grandchildren she will never have, or faces a repair without a man around to help take care of her. God understands this loss and calls the church to reduce the pain and loss for widows in their difficulty (James 1:27).

For Carol, it is not "I should forgive God, but . . .". Now it is, "I will trust God and accept these losses through His love."

I shared with her two final concepts that helped her understand her future. First, she would probably relive the losses she experienced, but the pain would not be as deep as it was in the past. Secondly, she would have triggers that recalled the losses, but the pain would not last as long. As time and maturity in Christ continue, the depth and duration of pain will lessen. There will always be a low-grade sense of loss. But, if we let it, it will deepen our walk with the Lord Jesus and increase our desire to be with Him (Phil. 1:21).

Carol did not need to bury the proverbial hatchet with God. He Himself had already been buried in the bowels of the earth in a borrowed tomb. He had already paid the ultimate price to reconcile us to Himself and bring us peace within. He lives today not for combat but to comfort us in our losses (2Cor. 1:4). He sent His Spirit to minister to us in our pain not to prevent pain (John 14:16). Carol switched from bitter attacks to blessed acceptance. For her, it is now well with her soul.

◊

Joy's losses did not come later in life. For her, they were there from day one. She had been bitter from such an early age that it became her total identity.

157

Chapter 10

"I'm Not the Forgiving Kind!"

Joy curled her legs up under herself as she sat in her floral, overstuffed chair. She cradled the side of her face in the palm of her right hand, resting her elbow on the arm of the chair. Up to this point I had used every insight, approach, or appeal I could think of to help Joy release her bitterness.

"Could it be that you feel you have to forget if you forgive?" She shrugged her shoulders.

"Are you afraid of letting yourself feel the anger?" Her quick piercing stare told me that was not it. I was scrambling.

"Would it make a difference to you if we could somehow make them pay dearly for what they did to you?"

Her eyes darted to the ceiling. She heaved a sigh and shook her head.

Missed again.

Then, as if out of the clear blue sky, she declared, "I guess I should forgive, but I'm just not a forgiving person." She glared again at the beige carpet, hoping that this declaration would end the conversation.

I have heard this despairing statement of resignation

159

many times through the years. At this juncture I wanted to draw her attention pointedly to her codified bitterness and insist that she deal with it in a biblical fashion immediately. Even the apostle Paul counseled his son in the faith to be ready at a moment's notice to reprove, rebuke, and exhort those to whom he was ministering. But one short phrase governed it all: Do it "with great patience and instruction" (2 Tim. 4:2). To the Thessalonians he said, " . . . admonish the unruly, encourage the fainthearted, help the weak, be patient with all men" (1 Thess. 5:14). True, in time the forgiveness must be addressed. But God used Joy to teach me even deeper reasons that make it hard for some to forgive.

Joy was saying volumes to me in that short cryptic statement, "I'm not the forgiving kind." She was defining for me who she was.

IDENTITY IN BITTERNESS

While in seminary I had a rude awakening about myself. I had winged it so well through college, but I could no longer do so. I was now taking Greek, or I should say, Greek was taking me.

The professor covered the various parts of speech in Greek grammar. I was struggling. Finally I could deny it no longer, I just did not know English grammar. It finally hit me, I was taking two "foreign" languages at one time, Greek and English, my mother tongue.

It was during one of these grueling grammar lessons, I learned a unique feature about the verb "to be." The professor said that the verb *eimi*, the English equivalent of "to be" acts like an equal sign. Whatever is said before this verb equals what follows it. I can say "the car is red" and the sentence makes sense. I could also say "red is the car," and it, too, would make sense. I began to listen to people's conversation when they used this verb. It was amazing to me what I learned.

One day, Helen bragged a little at a staff luncheon about her son being a terrific soccer player. And indeed he is. I thought about that statement: "My son is a good soccer player." It could be reversed, and stated like this: "A good soccer player is my son!" Is means "equals." Then I thought, "If her son's whole life identity equals soccer, who would he be if he broke his leg and could no longer play soccer?"

Identity equals value. Most of us draw our identity from what we do (e.g., play soccer) or what position we hold (e.g., president, mother, doctor, or soccer player).

Ideally it would be better for Helen to say, "John is (equals) my son, who plays soccer." Why? Because if John ever stops playing soccer he is still Helen's son! His performance does not change his position or relationship, just as our performance does not change our position in Christ when we fail (2 Tim. 2:13).

I am told that an identity crisis is the number one root cause of alcoholism among retired professional athletes. Their life (identity) is as a professional athlete. Upon retirement, if adequate preparation is not made, an identity crisis occurs. They cannot handle not being a much sought after professional athlete.

This not only is experienced by athletes, but by men whose identity is their job. Many men die soon after retirement because work was their purpose for living. Their job was who they were.

Our value is in direct proportion to whom or to what

we identify. It may not be a particular problem to identify with one's work or role. But what happens when our identity is pain or bitterness? This was the case with Joy. When she said she was not a forgiving person, she could as easily have said "a forgiving person I am not." This is where forgiveness becomes very difficult for a person who has made anger or bitterness their identity in response to physical or emotional hurts and losses in life.

It was at this point God led my mind back to the dark times in the Old Testament during the period of the judges, specifically to Bethlehem.

"CALL ME MARA"

Two journey-worn women trudged the dusty road to the outskirts of Bethlehem. Soft gasps could be heard everywhere, as women left their kneading bowls, stopped grinding their grain, and abandoned their baking ovens. Slowly at first, but picking up speed, they darted out to meet the unescorted women. But all eyes widened in amazement and perplexity at the older of the two women. To one another, in barely audible voices, they exclaimed, "Is this Naomi?"

It had been ten years since someone resembling her left Bethlehem during the severe famine with her husband, Elimelech, and two sons, Mahlon and Chilion. Her face and her walk looked very familiar, and yet . . . The muffled voices stopped abruptly. Naomi, her face etched deeply with grief, stood erect and sternly addressed the perplexed women, "Do not call me Naomi." The women gasped, almost in unison, clasping their hands over their mouths. "Call me Mara, for the Almighty has dealt very bitterly with me." Eyes darted back and forth at each other.

Naomi said it all in two short sentences: "I went out [from Bethlehem] full [having a husband and two grown sons], but the Lord has brought me back empty." (They died in the land of Moab.) In bitterness of spirit she chided the shocked bystanders: "Why do you call me Naomi [which in Hebrew means "sweetness" or "pleasantness"], since the Lord has witnessed against me and the Almighty [Shaddai] has afflicted me?" (Ruth 1:19–21).

Naomi so internalized her anger and bitterness over the loss of her family and her security that she even changed her name to reflect her pain. "Afflicted I was; bitter I am. Bitterness is me. It is who I am." Naomi wanted every occasion that her new name was used to be a reminder to herself and to others that she was the personification of bitterness. However, we have no record that her friends, or God, accepted her name change. She pictured for herself only bitterness when God, in fact, had prepared for her blessing.

Bitterness and anger make us myopic in outlook. Standing in the middle of the same dusty road stood a young widow—Naomi's daughter-in-law, Ruth. In time, the ignored Ruth would play a key role in restoring hope, security, and blessing to both. Bitterness blinds, but belief brightens. And in the working out of God's sovereign plan, even Naomi would come to say that God "has not withdrawn his kindness to the living and to the dead" (Ruth 2:20). But now, Naomi had codified her bitterness just like Joy had. Although Joy herself was blessed with three beautiful children and an outstanding Christian husband, she was still stuck in bitterness. Joy's confession, "I'm not the forgiving kind," revealed at least five facets about herself and her past that made it hard for her and others like her to forgive.

THE DURATION OF THE HURT

Joy was raised in a Christian home. Both parents had a personal relationship with Jesus Christ from their youth. Joy's mother was raised in a home filled with verbal warfare and criticism. She was alienated emotionally, and she learned to deal with it by shutting down her emotions, becoming a perfectionist—a critic of herself and an arch critic of others. That included her daughter, Joy. This was Joy's environment from day one. Joy felt early on that she could never please her mom or measure up to her expectations.

Joy was shamed for having any negative emotions and disciplined for these "bad attitudes." Anger was one of them. Just like Sally in chapter 2, if Joy expressed anger, she was disciplined. It never dawned on her mother that Joy may have had a legitimate hurt or offense that needed to be addressed. The message was clear to Joy: "Your anger and hurts are not important, and you must just learn to live with them."

Live with them? Yes. The sad part of this training is that she did just that. She learned to live with the anger and bitterness and they became a part of her, her very identity, who she was. If you choose to live with your anger, you are never able to send it away (to forgive). You keep it, and it becomes a part of you. Over time, anger will come to feel normal, even comfortable. No need to address it. It's not just a part of you now; it is you. Why change now?

If Joy's mother was law, then Dad was grace. But her dad had also contributed to Joy's pain of rejection. In her early years, he was the youth pastor of a very large church. Time demands were unmerciful. Then he joined a national seminar ministry—banker's hours. That is, when he was not on the road coordinating seminars. As the ministry van picked up the staff to take them to the airport, it would pick up her dad right at the front door. As he hugged young Joy and said good-bye, she sobbed and begged her dad not to leave. He would be gone for at least a week.

Dad was fun. He would play. They did things together. But he was gone. The feelings of abandonment plunged deep but did not remain only in childhood—they lasted well into her teen years. It was not safe to acknowledge the anger toward her critical mother or the hurt from her abandoning father. She would just have to live with it, stuff it, and keep it. And she did. It became an integral part of her, of who she was. It became her identity. She was the personification of the axiom, "if you cannot acknowledge emotional suffering and pain, you cannot heal it." You can't send it away (forgive). Instead you keep it! In time, anger and bitterness become as much a part of you as the color of your eyes or the shape of your nose. Anger is who you are. Joy reasoned "Yes, I should forgive, but that is just not me." To forgive meant that Joy would have to change who she was and, that was not going to happen, at least not yet.

THE DEPTH OF THE PAIN

Not only did Joy's statement about not being a forgiving person reveal the duration of her lifelong hurt, but also its depth. And the depth only compounded her difficulty to forgive.

Her critical mother had unintentionally conveyed, "You are defective and there is nothing you can do right. Failure is your destiny, and the fear of failure is to be your lot in life." This only drove Joy's anger deeper and now coupled it with fear.

There are few mental tortures that equal the torments that produce fear. For Joy, it was as if she lived on a high, swaying tightrope; she lived with the constant fear that at any moment she could slip (fail) and plummet to an instant painful death (rejection). This pain of ultimate rejection from imminent failure motivated her to do two things. First, she reasoned consciously, "Do not take risks. Withhold. Hide. Don't venture out. Avoid every potential threat." Her very survival depended on it. Second, she said to herself, "Since you are going to fall (fail) and be killed (rejected) anyway, just get it over with. Do it yourself." And she did. Joy sabotaged herself often. She would procrastinate doing her school assignments, which were not done very well. But she told herself if only she had had more time she could have done a better job. It was a time issue in her mind, not a character or ability flaw.

Perfectionism became her way of life. You may wonder, "How is perfectionism a reflector of fear and anger?" Simple. Perfectionists, to a greater or lesser degree, live in fear—the fear of discovery and subsequent rejection, which culminates ultimately in abandonment. Living with the fear that others may at any moment see a flaw and reject them only reinforces life on the tightrope. The netless cement floor one-hundred feet below only ratchets up the paralyzing fear. What does this have to do with anger? Joy was angry for who she was and bitter against those who set her up for it. The anger and fear lived just under the emotional surface, and it did not take much to set her off. When she walked around it was as if the proverbial cloud of anger and fear followed her, overshadowing all she did.

Joy's resigned statement, "But I'm not a forgiving person," revealed something further—a deep despair.

THE DESPAIR OF THE PAIN

"Christians should live in victory every day, and never experience despair." This was her mother's motto. It sounds right. It feels right, but it is dead wrong. Wrong? Didn't the apostle John state in his first letter, "For whatever is born of God overcomes the world; and this is the victory that has overcome the world—our faith" (1 John 5:4).

If having total victory without moments of despair is truly possible, and if the apostle Paul is any role model of the Christian experience, then we have a problem. Why? In one of his many moments of humble honesty, he revealed to the Corinthian church, "For we do not want you to be unaware, brethren, of our affliction which came to us in Asia, that we were burdened excessively [passive verb], beyond our strength, so that we despaired even of life" (2 Cor. 1:8).

Hopeless. We are not going to make it. It's over. There will be no change. Despair. As Naomi stood in the dusty road of Bethlehem, this, too, was her attitude. This is where Joy was. Nothing seemed to change. As hard as she would try, nothing changed. And even worse, no matter how hard she sought to please others, no one else was changing either. "This is permanent. It's me. It's real. I am an angry person and . . . yes, I guess this makes me an unforgiving person, too."

Despair is like glue. The longer it sets, the more permanent it becomes. She was going to stay with the super glue of despair, until someone entered her dark, bleak world and patiently led her out to the light of God's truth, through and by His grace. Not only did Joy's declaration reveal the duration of her hurt, the depth of her anger and the utter despair of her heart, it also revealed her means of avoiding forgiveness: bitterness became her defense from further hurts.

THE DEFENSE FROM PAIN

What is the purpose of a scab? The coagulation of blood quickly forms over an open wound for a purpose. First, it is to create an environment of healing, and second, to protect the wound from further infection while it heals.

Emotional scabs do the same. They give you time to heal. They fend off any further germs (offenses) from increasing the pain. One indication of the presence of an emotional scab is defensiveness. When Joy said, "I'm not a forgiving person," it was said as a defensive shield as much as an identity of character. "Let me alone. This is who I am. Bug off."

Joy's defensiveness showed itself in other ways. Joy felt she needed to defend herself against the smallest slights. Any statement resembling even the faintest bit of criticism met with an overkill of defensiveness. Her defensiveness became her best offense. Some would call her explosive reactions an overreaction. In reality, however, they were not overreactions but an accumulative reaction over the years.

Defensiveness only compounded Joy's difficulty with forgiveness. How? First, she could never admit being wrong herself; therefore, she would never experience receiving personal forgiveness. And second, as a result, she never felt motivated to grant it. It is very hard to give what you feel you never received. Wasn't Joy a Christian? Yes. Her mother led her to Christ as a small child. It is important to remember that we can be genuinely born again in our spirit and still struggle with issues of life in our mind (John 3:6; Rom. 12:2). It is also crucial to bear in mind that we can stay stuck emotionally and often spiritually at the points of our greatest hurts. Apparently, this is one reason the Apostle Paul honestly admitted, "And I, brethren, could not speak to you as

to spiritual men, but as to men of flesh as to babes in Christ."
Why? Because "there is jealousy and strife among you" (1
Cor. 3:1, 3). You are adults physically, but you are acting out
the behaviors of children, fighting over possessions, or in this
case, position, and defending your identity (v. 4): "I am of
Paul," or "I am of Apollos."

Defensiveness leads to the fourth characteristic of Joy's
identity with unforgiveness—the need for distance.

THE DISTANCE FROM PAIN

I vividly remember falling from a scaffold and landing
on and crushing my elbow. That hurt. I guarded that elbow
for weeks following my orthopedic surgery. "Don't even
think of getting close," was my motto. Not only did I protect it, I avoided close association to prevent unintentional
contact with my injury.

This is fine if it's an elbow. Appropriate protection is
called for. But if your whole life is in this protective mode,
it will also be a distant, lonely life.

Joy did just that. You could hurt her or offend her once.
That did it. It was not three strikes and you're out. It was
one offense and that was it. She could do this with casual
strangers and get away with it. But what if it was her husband, to say nothing of the kids? Tragically, they all paid
dearly. The sad part of a permanent defensive posture is that,
though few people will score against you, ultimately you still
lose the game. Why? Because it's only when you go on offense
that you score points. Only when you leave the defensive
position and take on the offensive position does life get better. The Apostle Paul expressed it this way: "Do not be overcome by evil (defense), but overcome evil with good (offense)"

(Rom. 12:21). It does not mean that you let evil overrun you. Rather, it means that instead of defending yourself against your opponent, you go on the offensive and "get the better of evil by doing good" (MOFFATT). What better good is there than forgiving the offenders in your life, taking back control of your life, and celebrating your freedom?

The "one-strike-and-you're-out" people take on a related identity that makes forgiveness very hard—they become the "victim."

DESTINED TO BE HURT

Joy's radar was always on—not to avoid traffic patrolmen, but to identify and avoid new or repeated offenders. Every word, action, and attitude expressed by others was scrutinized for a possible offense by a victim. If it is not an overt offense, it is a covert one. Innocent things are even mentally skewed into an offense.

Life normally has its offenses. Jesus said in this life you will have tribulation (John 16:33). The apostle James went so far as to challenge us to consider painful intrusions into our life as a source of joy and not to resent them as intruders into our otherwise peaceful life (James 1:2).

But Joy's identity as an unforgiving person set her up to be a career victim. Why? The logic is simple. "I have been hurt all my life. Nothing ever changes. I will get hurt again. It's only a matter of time. I am now back on that tightrope of fear again. This time someone is going to knock me off. This latest offense only proves I was right."

What Joy did not realize was that instead of viewing herself as a victor in Christ, she saw herself as a victim in life. Each normal conflict of life was like a slap on a lobster-red sunburn. Normally a good-natured slap on the back would be greeted as a friendly gesture. But to a career victim, it is construed as an intentional hurt.

It is virtually impossible for a lifestyle victim to forgive just as it is for a seasoned warrior, who has only known war, to bury the hatchet. Peace is awkward, uncomfortable, even boring. This explains why some veterans who leave the military become mercenaries for other countries. The adrenaline rush of war, fighting, and combat is so much a part of them that they have to prolong the battle—with anyone—because that is who they are. For a career victim, any offense is only validation of their core belief system that people are out to get them. Every offense just proves they were right. Evidence collecting is a different mind set than offense forgiving. Forgiveness means "to send away." A victim collects, catalogues, and stores offenses. Forgiveness identifies the offense and the offender and sends them away to the Jesus jail. Forgiving people have a small trunk. Victims pull a forty-foot tractor trailer rig. One maneuvers life easily, the other needs a large berth to navigate. Some people would not be as honest as Joy in admitting they are just not the forgiving type. Al was one of these.

IT'S JUST ME

When Al reluctantly came in with his wife for marriage counseling, it did not take long to find out at least one cause of the marital disharmony. Al had a temper. If confronted directly, Al would say he was generally a forgiving man. Why? It would be too sinful not to be forgiving. To admit to being unforgiving would bring on feelings of condemnation and shame. Through the years I have seen that high profile angry people, who even sheepishly concede they have a temper, are in reality unforgiving. They will not say they are an angry person in terms of their identity; they just say they have a temper. They disassociate from their anger, but in reality they are ("equal") angry people and are basically unforgiving. How do you know? Their temper is usually accumulative anger that has amassed over the years. Therefore, they are keepers of offenses (bitter), not senders of offenses (forgiving).

Al would not own up to his bitter identity. He kept saying it was something he did, not someone he is—bitter and unforgiving.

It is hard for a person to see or admit the depth of their own anger. They will hide it in the pursuit of possessions or position. Paul rebuked Simon for trying to purchase the power of the Holy Spirit and went to the root of his problem: "For I see that you are in the gall of bitterness and in the bondage of iniquity" (Acts 8:18, 23).

But just like Joy, Al wanted everyone, including his wife, to accept that he just had a temper. That's just Al. Accept it. It's just the way I am ("equal"). Live with it!

Now we are back to my English lesson. The "is" word means "equals." "I am an angry person; I have been this angry for years. It is not a part of me, in reality it is me." This elementary grammar lesson has helped me to identify what some people are doing to themselves that causes them to hold onto their emotional pain, making it next to impossible to forgive.

ANGRY CHURCH

I was visiting the home of a dear friend. He had a retired missionary couple visiting him. Linda and I were invited over to enjoy an evening of fellowship with them. After forty years of a faithful church-planting ministry, he and his wife were doing interim pastoral work for churches who were seeking a full-time minister.

It was while he was sharing his current church experience that he paused in mid-sentence, "You know what surprised me, Chuck? All the people who look you right in the face and tell you they are very forgiving. Then, only a few minutes later, they get lathered up in anger over a church split that happened twenty years ago. Now, how do you explain that?"

Perhaps Al could do it better than I. It is safer and more acceptable to display a little anger from time-to-time than to admit that you are not a forgiving person. True, Joy forgave no one. One strike and you're out. For Al it was two strikes and you're out. More seasoned relationship players may allow three, or even four strikes. The net result is the same. They all have a variation in their tolerance of offenses. But they also have an offense threshold, a limit. This far and no more.

The game that Jesus played allowed each player at least 490 strikes (seventy times seven). The only person that could play that long would have to make some changes. They would have to make deep changes. They would have to go to the very core of who they are. They would have to change their equation. It would mean an identity switch.

WHO IS?

I was discussing this chapter with a longtime friend and author, Norm Wright. When I mentioned the title of this chapter, "I'm Not the Forgiving Kind!" Norm rolled his eyes and shot back, "Who is?" His brief statement spoke volumes. Norm is a widely published author of books designed to help believers work through problems in living from a biblical perspective, with over sixty-five titles to his credit. He is a licensed family counselor. What has almost forty years of counseling, pastoring, teaching, writing, and research taught him? Who is forgiving? This does not imply that no one at any time ever forgives completely. But the implied meaning is simple. Everyone has pockets of unforgiveness or the potential not to forgive. It is hard for everyone—even the "who's who" of Scripture.

KING DAVID

One of my favorite biblical characters is King David. His name means "beloved." Bar none, he is the greatest king of Israel. I have personally visited his alleged tomb site in Jerusalem. It is the most venerated site in Israel, second only to the temple site. He is the second most mentioned man in Scripture, next to our Lord Jesus Christ.

Some of David's most significant accomplishments lie in the sphere of literature. Of the 150 canonical psalms, 73 have titles that assert his authorship. Yet David fell morally. He tried to cover up his adultery with Bathsheba by having her husband, Uriah, one of his best warriors, killed. But David received divine forgiveness—a total act of mercy and grace on God's part (2 Sam. 11–12).

Yes, as a result of his adultery, he lost control of his sons. Amnon followed his father's footsteps and raped his half sister, Tamar (2 Sam. 13:1–14). Absalom avenged Tamar by killing Amnon (2 Sam. 13:23–29). Absalom rebelled and drove his father out of Jerusalem. David went up the ascent of the Mount of Olives sobbing as he went, his head covered and his feet bare (2 Sam. 15:30).

As King David approached the city of Bahurim, loud shouts and cursing could be heard coming from the hillside. Shimei, from the family lineage of Saul and a resident of Bahurim, screamed loud curses and pelted King David and his escaping entourage. "Get out, get out, you man of bloodshed, and worthless fellow! The Lord has returned upon you all the bloodshed of the house of Saul, in whose place you have reigned; and the Lord has given the kingdom into the hand of your son Absalom. And behold, you are taken in your own evil, for you are a man of bloodshed" (2 Sam. 16:7–8). Abishai wanted to cut the head off of this "dead dog" that cursed the king. But David factored God into Shimei's deeds. "Let him alone and let him curse, for the Lord has told him. Perhaps the Lord will look on my affliction and return good to me instead of his cursing this day" (2 Sam. 16:9–12). King David turned Shimei over to God. Fast forward. On David's deathbed he gives his son Solomon his last wishes. The greatly forgiven man recalls with vividness the day he was cursed by Shimei and instructs his son, "And behold, there is with you Shimei . . . now it was he who cursed me with a violent curse on the day I went up to Mahanaim. But when he came down to me at the Jordan, I swore to him by the Lord, saying, 'I will not put you to death with the sword.'" Then a pocket of unforgiveness is exposed even in the heart of the great Psalmist of Israel: "Now therefore do not let him go unpunished, for you are a wise man; and you will know what you ought to do to him." To make sure there is no confusion as to what he meant, he concludes, " . . . and you will bring his gray hair down to Sheol with blood" (1 Kings 2:1–9).

How do we know that King David's request for revenge

probably did not please the Lord? Simple. As soon as Solomon ascended the throne, he humbly asked God to "give Thy servant an understanding heart to judge Thy people to discern between good and evil" (1 Kings 3:9). God's response? "And it was pleasing in the sight of the Lord that Solomon had asked this thing" (v. 10). Then, God revealed His heart's desire for a godly king: "Because you have asked this thing and have not asked for yourself long life . . . riches . . . nor have you asked for the life of your enemies . . . I have done according to your words" (vv. 11, 12).

Revenge was one of the last actors on King David's stage of life. David reflected a common human perspective: We want justice for others, but mercy for ourselves. David could not trust God for justice and grant forgiveness.

Does this thrust for revenge rob King David of his title as a man after God's own heart? No. As a man of faith? No. But it punctuates with clarity for us all how hard it is to forgive, and that even the greatest of the greats have failed this very hard discipline of the faith. That is why Norm Wright's words ring with reality: "Who is forgiving?" Who is characterized as totally forgiving in every way?

But King David's pocket of revenge—his weakness in the flesh—only served to jog my memory. It could happen to anyone. The apostle Paul cautioned the churches of Galatia, "Brethren, even if a man is caught in any trespass, you who are spiritual, restore such a one in a spirit of gentleness; each one looking to yourself, lest you too be tempted" (Gal. 6:1). Another translation nails it down, " . . . keeping an attentive eye on yourself, lest you should be tempted also" (AMPLIFIED BIBLE). Tempted to do what? Among other things, tempted to urge others to forgive while secretly harboring pockets of unforgiven hurt yourself.

FROM THE BEGINNING

Where did Joy's journey to freedom begin? I temporarily laid aside the "should" of forgiveness. Forgiveness is the destination for Joy, not the beginning. I asked her a simple question: "Would you be willing to start from the very beginning of your life, as early as you can remember, and share with me your personal painful journey?" Her sarcastic glance said, "And you care?" Ignoring her look, I asked again, "Would you be open to share it with me?"

It is important to remember that a long-term bitter person trusts no one outside themselves. Trust is earned, not demanded. Joy tried many times to get me to give up on her. Honestly, I struggled with just that. I have realized over the years that not everyone is open for help and healing. I wondered if she was "one of those."

But a few important truths ring in my mind daily: "I am not responsible for their change, they are." I cannot fix them; only they can through the grace of God. I am not omniscient and do not know who will respond—just like I do not know who will be saved as a result of my witness to the claims of Christ. Just as I am to sow and water with the Word of God and pray that an unsaved person will respond, I sow and water with the Scripture, praying others will respond in obedience and be healed of past hurts.

"I am willing to listen . . . are you open to share?" The offer was repeated in many ways. Why was this necessary? Simple. God documents the fact that "a brother offended is harder to be won than a strong city" (Prov. 18:19). I am attacking a well-fortified castle. I have seen crusader castles in the Middle East and some of the great fortresses in Europe. Each had incredible creative devices to prevent hostile forces from penetrating cleverly devised defenses. But one feature they had in common. Each of them fell at one time or another. In my heart, this was my hope for Joy.

She started. Testing me at every paragraph. My eyes rarely left hers. The other female staff member who sat in with me prayed silently. This was not a physical battle. This was a jihad—*a spiritual battle* (Eph. 6:12).

Why did I have her start from the beginning? She did not have to, but most people automatically start there because that's where they begin to weave a story. Disjointed at times, yes. Nonetheless, it is God's responsibility to bring up whenever and whatever He wants to their minds. But I had another reason for starting there. I wanted her to identify every hurt and offense she could. As she talked, I made note of every offense, and who did it. Why? Because in time, when God brings her to a place of starting the forgiving process, we will have it all noted and can then begin to go through each offense and forgive the offenders.

She would share one, and I would acknowledge the hurt. Then I would say, "Tell me another one." When she sensed it was safe, and she would not be judged or shamed, she would go to the next one.

One might question at this point, "Why let her vent her anger and bitterness? What good is that going to do? It is just going to stir things up and make the anger deeper. What purpose will it serve?"

First, the word vent has been used and abused. Joy may think she is just "venting," getting things off her chest, airing her feelings publicly. I have found through the years this usually gives only temporary relief, not long-range closure. Do not view this part of the process of "telling her story" as an end in itself. It is only a means to an end. The ultimate aim is to bring these issues to the throne of grace, transfer the offender over to the Lord Jesus Christ, and be released from the bondage of anger and bitterness. But there is a real problem if you ignore or by-pass this important step. If you do not know what to forgive, how are you going to forgive? Just as an orthopedic surgeon looks at an X-ray before he operates, so we too must find out how deep the wound is, and where it is, before we start the surgical process toward healing.

Usually, exploratory surgery is much harder on a patient than targeted surgery. Even God warns us about answering a matter before we hear it: "He who gives an answer before he hears [gets an X-ray], it is folly and shame to him" (Prov. 18:13). Plus, if the disease can be located precisely, a lot of unnecessary discomfort can be avoided. View the telling of one's story as an X-ray, a necessary part in preparation for a serious surgical procedure.

CLARIFY THE OFFENSE

As Joy unfolded her story, she did not pause, and say, "Now this is precisely how I was hurt." She just told her story. "When my parents would always favor my younger sister," Joy explained, "I thought 'what's wrong with me?'"

"It hurt you that they favored your younger sister over you?" I queried.

"Yeah, like all the time."

That is called favoritism or partiality. God wants us to acknowledge differences (weak, strong), but love without partiality (James 2:9).

Some may say, "But that was just her perception; they did not intend to hurt her." It is important to understand in people-helping that both a deliberate gunshot and an accidental gunshot feel the same. One would not feel better in the hospital emergency room with a fatal wound thinking, "It really does not hurt because it was an accident." Furthermore, a perceived offense feels the same as an actual offense. My goal was not to defend, explain, justify, or minimize what was done to her—it was for Joy to identify the offense so that she could in time apply the precious blood of Christ to that wound, forgive the offenders, and glorify the Father through it all.

On the other hand, minimization of another's pain causes the wounded one to withdraw, stuff their feelings, and ignore the offense. As a result, they ignore the use of the badly needed biblical tool of forgiveness. It is hard to forgive what you were told should not have hurt you anyway. That is why I encouraged Joy to "tell it all." Again, you cannot heal what you will not acknowledge. Now we are back to our definition of Christian denial: "Denying God access to a hurt He wants to heal for our benefit and for His glory."

Two of the best things you can do to help someone struggling to forgive is to let them tell their story and help them pinpoint the offense. Everyone is willing to tell their story for the purpose of enlisting sympathy. They may be chronic complainers looking for a listening ear. But once you can get them to acknowledge the specific offense, you are ready for step two!

WHAT ARE THE OPTIONS?

From Joy's perspective, she had three options: to be bitter, to be bitter, or to be bitter. You may think, they are all the same! You are right. In Joy's mind, she had only one choice. Nancy felt the same: "I should forgive, but I can't forget." Sally thought, "I can't admit I'm angry, so I can't acknowledge a wrong, so I can't forgive." Fred made it clear,

"I can't forgive because my dad would get off scot-free. He needs to pay." These are just some of the reasons that make it hard to forgive. But each one was given other options to handle their hurt. What was Joy's option? The key was in the duration and depth of pain.

"Joy, how long have these things hurt you?"

"How long is forever?" she snapped back.

"How long do you want to keep hurting?"

"Like I have a choice!" she bolted back sarcastically.

"Would you be surprised to know that you do?"

"Am I about to get a sermon?" she retorted.

"You're twenty-nine years old. It's my opinion you have suffered long enough!"

She quickly turned her head to the wall and stared at it, attempting to avoid the confusion churning in her mind. Confusion? Often a person will say they feel confused when faced with this and other hard choices. Confusion is the collision of at least two important elements: feelings and facts.

"I know what's right . . . I . . . I know this in my mind . . . but I don't feel it will work."

"Joy, it's time. It's time to choose what you know is right and good for you. Obedience is good for you. It is the doorway to blessing. Every way you turn now, it's lose, lose. I believe it's time to win. Jesus came that you might have life and have it more abundantly. But the first part of that verse seems to describe you: "Now, the thief comes only to steal, kill, and destroy" (John 10:10).

WHO WOULD I BE?

We were so close that I could almost sense her forming a prayer on her lips. Then she hit me with this bomb: "If I did this, I wouldn't know who I was. I've always been this unforgiving person." I personally would not have guessed that an identity crisis would make it hard for a person to forgive, until now. Joy was going to have to be willing to make a major identity shift as a result of her forgiveness.

FOR ME TO LIVE—CHRIST

For years I would quote to myself and others the apostle Paul's declaration of identification with Christ: "For to me, to live is Christ, and to die is gain" (Phil. 1:21). It certainly had meaning for me, but not until I translated it from the Greek did I began to understand the thrust of this verse. I discovered the word "is" was not in the Greek text, but had been added for clarity by the translators. And, for impact, the verb *eimi* ("to be") is absent. Paul is stressing his close identity to Christ by saying, "For me to live—Christ." Paul was so intimate in his relationship with Christ that he was able to tell his contemporaries to follow him as he followed Christ (2 Thess. 3:7).

Why is this concept so important in overcoming the difficulty in forgiving? Simple. Our Lord Jesus is the only absolute forgiver. Therefore, our ability to forgive is in direct proportion to our genuine identity with Him. Or, to say it in a negative way, our reluctance to forgive reflects the distance in our relationship with Christ. The apostle John reveals the real issue: "If someone says, 'I love God,' and hates his brother, he is a liar; for the one who does not love his brother whom he has seen, cannot love God whom he has not seen" (1 John 4:20).

If Joy forgives, who is she going to be? She hit the nail on the head. She recognized she had identified with a behavior (anger) instead of a person (Jesus). It was time to begin to make the switch. That she did, but not in front of me.

It was at an intense three-day spring retreat that she broke through the barriers of anger, bitterness, and identity. Two incredible changes transpired. First, she forgave her husband for not living up to her standard of perfection and for the normal mistakes he made as a young groom. Second, she now grants a greater amount of grace to herself and to others—both past and present. It's no longer the one-strike-and-you're-out mentality. She reported later that the frequent domestic battles had all but disappeared. Do they still have normal challenges? Yes. But now, free from the prison of anger and bitterness, she has now transferred her identity to Christ. She is reflecting His character and enjoying the difference.

What about her parents? After forgiving her mother for her overbearing control, criticism, and emotional aloofness, a freeing insight hit her. Mom was acting out her own unresolved issues. This fresh perspective unlocked the door to compassionate understanding. Forgiveness opened the door and compassion walked through it.

What about Dad? Joy chose to release him, too, through forgiveness. But now she is confronted with what to do after forgiving her husband and her parents. With her core belief system changed as to who she is, how should she now act when she is around them? How should she respond to them? How are they going to respond to her?

◊

Andrew and Lori had this and more in common with Joy. But one specific fear that they were unwilling to face kept them from forgiving.

Chapter 11

"I Can't Let Go!"

H i, *Chuck and Linda*," came a friendly voice from the next table.

"Anne. Mike. Good to see you both. How have you folks been?"

"We're doing great. Did you know our son, Andrew, is coming in to see you tomorrow? He is ready to unload all his junk."

"I'll look forward to seeing him. Good to see you. Enjoy your meal."

Incredible! This is a miracle. Miracle? I rarely get to experience this phenomenon. Here is a mom and dad who have worked through many serious family and marital issues and are now enjoying the fruit of their hard work. But something else has happened. That is what is incredible. Their dental-student son was ready to begin his journey of allowing God to heal his aching soul.

I honor Anne and Mike. They were bold enough to face their past and present. Their kids were watching and saw their parents change. The kids, too, had been damaged and hurt. By Mike and Anne allowing God to bring healing in their lives, they, by example, gave permission to their kids to turn to God with their hurts.

PERMISSION?

We have discussed issues that make it hard for different ones to forgive. Those are common issues. But a hindrance that often makes it hard to forgive is the feeling that we do not have permission even to look at past events. The unbiblical, dysfunctional Christian family still lives by three rules: Don't feel. Don't trust. And, for heaven's sake, don't tell anybody! It is a test of loyalty to keep the family secret at all costs. Their family pride is fragile at best. It cannot sustain anymore losses. But Mike and Anne broke the code of silence and marched into freedom.

You will remember that the past that is not processed still keeps surfacing and causing conflict in the present. Mike and Anne were painfully aware of their past. They both grew up in homes that codified the "Three Rules." But something happened. The relational pain had escalated to unbearable heights, and a scream sprang up from their souls, "No more!!! Enough is enough." Then they sought out help.

It was my honor to serve them. But what they may not have understood at the time was that the three children were looking on, watching Mom and Dad break through many of those dysfunctional roles. They saw them grow in Christlikeness, and everyone experienced the benefits.

Andrew was the oldest. He loved and respected his parents. "If they can do it and survive, I can," he reasoned. By Mom and Dad's example, they gave Andrew permission to look, feel, trust, and best of all, to share. But this is not normal. The common pattern is for Mom and Dad to hide, ignore, or block out their pain. By doing so, they deny God access to their pain. They remain in the prison of their pain.

The apostle Paul boldly stated, through the inspiration of the Holy Spirit what Christ came to do in us. "It was for freedom that Christ set us free" (Gal. 5:1). Free from what? First, from our sin, so that we could begin a fresh relationship with Him. Second, from our former way of life, so that we could have a totally different life now—not just in the future. If God's singular goal was to save us from the consequences of our sin (hell), then He would have taken us all home to be with Him right after the point of salvation. But no! This is not the only reason for salvation. He fully intended for us to grow and reflect Christ in our life, here and now, not just in heaven. Look at the twenty-seven books of the New Testament. How much is devoted to explaining how to be saved? Less than 10 percent. The other 90 percent is teaching believers how to live as followers of Christ.

Mike, Anne, and Andrew were as born again as anyone will ever be. But it was time to be who they were called to be. The apostle Paul explained it this way: "For whom He foreknew, He also predestined to become conformed to the image of His Son" (Rom. 8:29). It is important to note that the words "to become" are not in the Greek text but were inserted by the translators. "Conformed" here is actually an adjective, not a verb. It is describing the "called one." In God's mind we are called "conformed."

But this creates a problem. I may be called "conformed," but I may not act or look conformed. This is where the balance of the 90 percent of Scripture comes in—to make what is a positional truth a practical reality. When Mike and Anne took the scary steps to face their past, it became God's tool to conform them into the image of Christ, and gave Andrew permission to do so as well.

LIFE'S NOT WORKING

I had known Andrew before he had entered his teen years. I watched him navigate through his punk rock, spiked, rainbow-colored hair stages. It was an honor to celebrate his graduation from college and to attend his Christ-centered wedding. Yet one day he sat in my office depressed. Life was not working for him.

"I have been battling this depression for a long time," Andrew began slowly. "It just seems to get worse."

"When did it seem to begin, or when did you become aware of it?"

"I guess after my spring semester. I had not been real busy, and I guess I started to do some thinking."

This is normal. Busyness is one form of emotional anesthesia. If we keep our minds active, we will not think. If we do not think, we will not feel. Often the painful emotions are the doorway to depression. I pressed him further.

"Andrew, what is the purpose of anesthesia?" Shrugging his shoulders he responded, "to deaden pain in order to perform some surgical procedure."

"Would you be open to share with me what you may be anesthetizing with your depression?" He took a deep breath, then forcibly exhaled into his clenched fist.

Andrew remembered the move his family made from Oregon to the Midwest. Before the move things seemed to be good. But the purpose of the move turned his world upside down. His father, who was a physician-in-training at the time, was to begin his residency. Those familiar with

medical training know this is a totally consuming experience. Real life stops for the student but not for his family.
Andrew missed his dad during those years.

"Dad was never there. To make it worse, he left me with
my neurotic mom. She was emotionally and physically abusive. She took her junk out on me. Dad was never there to
protect me. Even their relationship seemed to be falling apart."

The hurts began to reel off like a Gatling gun. "He was
not there as a father figure. Dad didn't support me in school
sports. I had to be responsible at an early age for my own
childhood. In fact, I don't even remember having one. I lost
a lot of confidence and self-worth because there was no rein-
forcement at home or school." His mind drifted to his mother.
"I missed a lot of love and affection from my mother. A big-
time loss was that my own home was not a safe place. It
seemed like a total loss of peace."

Tears trickled down his cheeks as his eyes stared distantly
out the window. He continued. "I'm almost too embarrassed
to admit it. It'll sound stupid, but it hurts me to see my dad
playing and relating to my siblings today. I mean I want him
to, but I wanted him to so badly then." The bitter anguish
shot to the surface. "He tried to make up for it, but it was
too late in the game—too little too late."

Now, many years later, life was not working for Andrew.

SOUNDS STUPID

When Andrew finished unloading I asked him, "What
do you mean by the word stupid?" This was a crucial
question. Why? Andrew watched his sister and brother inter-
act with his dad during family sports or board games. It was
fun. As an adult Andrew was happy to see them enjoying

their dad. They should. But something else was happening to Andrew. Their fun with Dad triggered his memories of what he had missed.

I experienced this type of response with my wife's aunt. The three of us stood on the north side of the Golden Gate Bridge overlook. The view of the San Francisco skyline was breathtaking. I held my wife's hand. Instantly Aunt Grace said, "Please don't hold hands in public. It hurts those of us who do not have someone to hold our hand." Her husband had died and our affection was a reminder of her loss.

Andrew, on one hand, responded as an adult, realizing his siblings should enjoy their Dad. But on the other hand there was a deep loss. He told me that the years between age five and eleven were the most painful of his life. The jealousy did not sound like a twenty-three-year-old; it sounded like a five-year-old. "Does the five-year-old in your memory resent your siblings for what they enjoy now?" I asked. His eyes clamped shut. The muscles in his jaws tightened as his teeth clenched. He nodded affirmingly. He was embarrassed and ashamed. I reminded Andrew that it was not stupid to the five-year-old in his memory. It was real. "Stupid" was the adult perspective of that hurt, not the child's perspective.

I had a specific reason for him to identify the pain at such a deep level. God explains that there are serious consequences if we do not forgive from the heart, the core of our being (Matt. 18:35). I wanted Andrew, when he was ready to forgive, to reach deeply inside his inner core, and release his father from the prison of anger and bitterness.

But before all this could happen, there was one more important step that would have to take place first.

FORGIVENESS CLARIFIED

"Andrew, would you be willing to lay all of this aside for a moment and clarify something for me?" In years past I would have pressed him to forgive his dad which, in itself, would not have been wrong. But what happens so often is that weeks or months later I would discover forgiveness did not actually take place. Why? Because what he thinks forgiveness is, and what God says it is, may be two separate things. Usually, any similarity between what most people think forgiveness is and what God says it is, is purely accidental. John was no exception.

"Andrew, from your perspective, would you tell me what you understand forgiveness to be?

His response was redundant, "Everyone knows it's just forgiving someone."

"Try it again," I insisted. It was déjà vu for me all over again. I have been here before. Andrew unknowingly explained why forgiveness is so hard for most. They confuse the results of forgiveness with forgiveness itself.

"Well, I guess it's when you feel better afterwards."

"Anything else?"

"It is when you do not think about it anymore. It doesn't come up in your thinking."

"Is that all?"

"Well, you kinda feel better and you can get a life and go on. It means you are having a better relationship with someone."

Others have said, "It's when I can be around the person and not want to kill them. . . . The anger seems to be gone. . . . I guess I can see they've got problems, too," or a related one. . . . "It is when you can see why they did it. . . . It's when you can be civil to each other. . . . When I realized they were not going to change. . . . I just got tired of the mess and gave it up."

More spiritual definitions run in this vein: "When I can love them again, or pray for them." Or the acid test is, "when I can work with them again." Or, "we are getting along better." Every one of these perceptions of forgiveness are all *results* of forgiveness, not a definition of it.

This phenomenon explains why many people say they forgave someone but that it did not work for them. When I hear this, I simply ask, "What didn't work for you?" They say, "forgiveness."

"What do you mean by forgiveness?" Bingo! Out come all those effects or results and they remain clueless as to God's meaning of forgiveness.

Just to illustrate the absurdity of their statements, let us use them as if God forgave us in like manner. When God forgives us (see 1 John 1:9):

He begins to feel better.
He just doesn't think about it anymore.
He is just getting a life and moving on.
He can stand to be around us without wanting to kill us.
He can see we have problems.
He can understand now why we sin.
He can act civilly toward us now.
He finally realizes we are not going to change.
He can now pray with us and work with us.

Ridiculous! When we forgive, we have to be doing the same thing He does. God does not use two different Greek words in the New Testament for forgiveness, one for Himself and the other for us. Whatever He does we do. Conversely, whatever we do must be consistent with His ways.

Andrew had been a Christian for years. He, too, had been exposed to a significant amount of Bible preaching and teaching. But he suffered from a very common lack in his Christian experience—ignorance as to the ways of God.

"Andrew, do you remember the Old Testament story of the scapegoat?"

"Yeah, sort of," came his ambivalent reply.

Ambivalent? This happens all the time. People have heard the word "scapegoat" and have some familiarity with it. It is usually negative. Someone is taking the rap, or blame for someone else. Ironically, this is close to its original meaning.

I reviewed for Andrew the account of the Old Testament priest casting lots for the two goats. The "winning" goat was to be killed as a sin offering. The "losing" goat was presented alive before the Lord to make atonement upon it, and then it was sent (led) into the wilderness and released as the scapegoat (Lev. 16).

The technical name for the goat was, "goat of removal." He was a figure of our Lord Jesus Christ, who took our sin and put it on Himself and then was killed (2 Cor. 5:21).

Forgiveness means "to send away," just like the goat that was sent (led) away with Israel's sin. John the Baptist, watching Jesus of Nazareth walking toward him, cried out in his fiery voice, "Behold, the Lamb of God who takes away the sin of the world!" (John 1:29).

"Andrew, when you were dating Alicia, did you ever send her a letter?"

"Sure. Plenty of times, while we were attending different colleges."

"How did you do it?" Remember, I'm asking this of a

straight "A" dental school scholar. Yet, may I remind you, it was he who had forgiveness confused, not me. There is a basic principle in pedagogy that states that basic learning takes place when you go from the known to the unknown. Andrew knows letter writing, but he does not understand forgiveness.

"Well, I write a letter, and I put it in the mail."

"I don't think it will go anywhere. What's missing?"

"Okay, I have to put it in an envelope, seal it, and mail it."

"It's still not going anywhere," I insisted.

In frustration, he blurted out, "All right, I put a stamp on it and even put my return address on it. It's gone!"

"Andrew, if you did that, that letter is going to come right back to you unopened. What have you omitted?"

"What's the point? I have to put an address on it," now his frustration has turned into disgust.

"You got it," I exclaimed.

This is the precise reason forgiveness substitutes do not work either. People acknowledge a hurt (write the letter), and want to get rid of it (put it in an envelope and drop it in a mailbox), but it comes right back to them. Why? No address! *The only legitimate recipient of our or others' sins is our Lord Jesus Christ.* When He was nailed to a Roman cross of execution, all our sin was nailed to it through His hands and feet. The apostle Paul explains to the believers in Colosse: " . . . and when you were dead in your transgressions and the uncircumcision of your flesh, He made you alive together with Him, [how] having forgiven us all our transgressions, [how] having canceled out the certificate of debt consisting of decrees against us and which was hostile to us; and He has taken it out of the way, having nailed it to the cross" (Col. 2:13, 14).

"Does this make sense to you, Andrew? It is a matter of listing your father's sins against you and sending them to Jesus or, as we have talked before, transferring him over to the 'Jesus jail'."

He was ready. He was going to do it. I could feel him moving right to the point of release and freedom. Then he dropped his bombshell.

BUT I CAN'T LET GO

Discouragement is no stranger to those who minister to people. Paul described his intense efforts: "My children, with whom I am again in labor until Christ is formed in you" (Gal. 4:19). Labor? Helping people to grow into Christlikeness is often tantamount to giving birth to a child. I have been in on the deliveries of both of my daughters and both of my grandchildren. The birthing was no picnic, for my wife, Linda, or my daughter, Dee Dee. And neither is spiritual warfare.

I asked Andrew pointedly if he was ready to release and forgive his dad. Sincerely and respectfully he said, "I know I should but I just don't want to give it up." Not want to give up his anger and bitterness? What possibly could not be clear? I had spent five sessions with him. Where did I miss it?

Almost forty years of entering into the spiritual struggles of others has taught me many things. One of these lessons was sitting across from me.

I thought I knew the meaning of each word Andrew spoke. But did I? After taking a deep breath, I did something I had done many times before. I asked him to clarify for me what appeared to him to be obvious. Why? It rarely is. Andrew shared the reasons for his reluctance to forgive. "If I forgive my father, and our relationship is restored, how do I then relate to him? And what if he hurts me again?" These just happen to be the same two reasons two bitter warriors will stand face to face in momentary silence before they each stoop down and bury their blood-stained tomahawks in the ground.

HOW SHALL I THEN LIVE?

"I bet you think I just don't want to forgive and get rid of this garbage," was his opening shot. "I hate it! The harder I push it down, the faster it comes up. But I have a problem, and it's not forgiveness. It's fear. I have related to my dad for over twenty-three years out of anger and bitterness. Okay! I forgive him. But how in the world do I relate to him now? I don't know if you get it, but I am clueless as to how to act socially as a son, friend, or anything else. Do you get it? I have to start at square one. Start over. Like relearn how to relate. It would be easier for me to have both legs and arms injured and have to learn to walk and use my arms again. I don't think you understand!" Every muscle in his body wanted to rush him out of my office. "Now you know. I'm scared spitless!"

The look on his face and his slumped shoulders said it all. "Shoot me and get it over with." No doubt many other men and women like Andrew have been "shot" by condemning words like, "Why don't you just grow up? Stop attending your own pity party. You know, you're only thinking of yourself. Don't blame others for your bad attitude."

Perhaps the apostle Paul could answer this best: "Let no unwholesome word proceed from your mouth, but only such a word as is good for edification according to the need of the moment, that it may give grace to those who hear" (Eph. 4:29). Notice the phrase "need of the moment." Andrew didn't need a rebuke. He already hurt and wanted to deal with it. He needed to hear how to do it. He did not need to be told how horrible he was for not doing it.

Men tend to learn better from stories. I asked Andrew if he minded if I told him a story of his clone, Lori. They were alike enough to be fraternal twins. His affirming nod seemed to come more out of curiosity than a desire to continue.

DYSFUNCTIONAL RERUN

Lori's family exhibited many of the same traits and dysfunctional roles as Andrew's family. There were a few notable exceptions. Her dad had at least two confirmed affairs as he traveled for his company, and he was a closet alcoholic. It was the family secret.

When Lori was pressed to forgive her parents, fear clouded her face. As with Andrew, I began to inquire of the common roadblocks prohibiting her from releasing her parents.

She knew she "should" forgive. This was not the issue. Finally, out of desperation I asked point-blank: "Why can't you forgive?" What God taught me through Lori has been a key to open up many closed hearts to obedience to God, and a final release for them.

The fear quickly switched to frustration. "You don't understand," her voice quivered in desperation. "What would I be like, or look like, or even act like if I was not bitter and angry? I was born and raised on a steady diet of anger. It's all I know. I wouldn't know how to relate to my parents. I don't think they would know how to respond to me."

Here is where many people-helpers get confused. They

confuse the "how to forgive" with the "ought to forgive." They focus entirely on the need to forgive so intently that they fail to listen for the roadblocks to forgiveness. But something emerged out of Lori's frustration that revealed another important key to forgiveness. She could not picture in her mind what the change would look like. Why was she so frustrated with me? Simple. I did not help her visualize life beyond bitterness.

LIFE AFTER BITTERNESS

My theologically trained mind began to argue with itself. Obedience must always come before understanding. This is true. I agree. But those who have been bitter their entire lives would not agree. God's Spirit is faithful to bring to our minds the Scripture at our point of need. I found myself acknowledging her need. Then as much as a surprise to me as it was to her, I acknowledged that her need shed some light on an important passage of Scripture. I believe God had this human frailty in mind as He inspired the apostle Paul to pen the doctrinal letter to the church of Rome.

Romans 12 starts with an all-encompassing appeal. It is costly. Life changing. Revolutionary. If obeyed there would be a total lifestyle change. Paul begins, "I urge you therefore, brethren, by the mercies of God to present your bodies a living and holy sacrifice, acceptable to God, which is your spiritual service of worship" (Rom. 12:1).

I asked Lori if she knew why the word "therefore" was in verse one. Her response was obvious. "I guess because of whatever he just said. "

"Brilliant! God just spent eleven chapters detailing His rich mercies to both the Jews and the Gentiles. There had to be a reason that God did not call for this total commitment in chapter 1 but waited until chapter 12. One reason, I believe, is obvious. It was Lori's question. It was Andrew's question: "Why should I do it, and what will it look like?"

How do you know you may ask? It appears to me that God had laid the foundation of this appeal with "why" information, and then detailed the "what" information in chapter 12. God did not leave the Roman believers in a vacuum. He took one verse for the appeal and the remaining twenty verses to flesh-out what life on the altar would look like. "Do not think of yourself more highly than you ought" (NIV). This is the attitude God wanted Lori to have in her family. Exercise your spiritual gift instead of seeking their approval. Why is this important? It is very logical. All Lori's life she, like a chameleon, was whatever others wanted her to be, whether it was Christlike or not.

God desires for us to get our identity totally in Christ. Then, He wants us to identify and focus on the use of our spiritual gift(s), both in our family and in God's family, the church. "Let love be without hypocrisy." This may include telling parents the truth in love. "Abhor what is evil." You do not have to like or accept their unbiblical, unhealthy behavior. "Cling to what is good." Attempt to focus on even the small good and appropriate things they do. This chapter is more than a survival guide. It is a strategy for victory. And if chapter 12 is not enough, the remaining four chapters of Romans only amplify in greater detail what is summarized in chapter 12.

Lori, like Andrew, was born again. For some people, the transformation at the point of salvation is abrupt and drastic. It's like day and night. But for most of us, the change is gradual and progressive. A paradigm shift must take place from being bitter and unforgiving to being obedient and forgiving. Lori, like Andrew, had been born again, but she needed now to learn how to live again after bitterness. Yes, for most, it is one thing to be born again and yet another to learn how to live again. But there is life after bitterness.

As I recounted Lori's journey, Andrew slowly shook his head from side to side in disbelief. It was written all over his face, "You mean I'm not the only one who thinks like this?" I do not know of a financial gift great enough to equal the relaxed relief that poured over his face. At the risk of an overkill, I began to end our session with an analogy he could relate to as a dental student.

ON THE MEND

The memories of my shattered elbow had not faded from my mind. I vividly remember the instructions my orthopedic surgeon gave to me. "Do not favor your injured elbow. Start doing arm curls immediately. Rest your arm on a table. Put a small can of food in your hand and curl it up to your shoulder." I thought to myself, "That's easy for you to say!"

Then he gave me his bottom-line warning: "If you don't do it yourself, I will send you to a physical therapist, and he will move it." The choice was not pain versus no pain. It was either I made myself do it or it was going to be done to me. The doctor then said to me with a touch of sternness, "You may want to do it yourself, if you know what I mean?"

But what if I didn't choose to do either? I already knew the answer. My arm would heal but in an unnatural position and not regain full use. It's sad, but this describes many broken, wounded people. They are now stuck in an unnatural way of living and not very useful to themselves or to others.

"Andrew, your emotional arm is broken. I have been like a cast around it (Gal. 6:1). The cast does not heal it, it only creates an environment for the arm to heal itself. It's time to forgive and begin the 'physical therapy.' It will be awkward for awhile, but I promise it will get well and the cast will soon come off. You will be whole."

We prayed. We went down his penciled list, reading off each offense on his lined notebook paper. Dad was transferred to the Jesus jail. Andrew was on the mend.

When this first issue of how to relate to his dad if he forgave him was addressed, the second issue of the possibility of being hurt by his father again became irrelevant to him.

◊

But reabuse wasn't irrelevant to Vicky. It almost froze her in her tracks. "What if I forgive my parents and they hurt me again?"

Chapter 12

"They'll Only Do It Again!"

I *don't know why I'm here,"* Vicky sighed in a discouraged
tone of voice. "I promised myself I would do this once.
No amount of counseling is going to change my family. I
wonder what's the use in trying. I'm not forgiving again. That
didn't work! They just keep hurting me."

I've found that most people like Vicky, who have gone
through the effort to make an appointment with a counselor or their pastor, or just to call a trusted friend, need
two things. Each one struggles inwardly alone first. Then
they hit a dead end, a brick wall. They're stuck. The hurt
remains high or continues to escalate. Circumstances go
from bad to worse. Vicky's heart was crying out for the two
ingredients found in the word comfort. And she needed
these before she was ready to tackle handling repeat offenders or to forgive again.

COMFORT

When the word comfort is cracked open like a walnut
shell, you quickly discover two important ingredients. The

first is hope when things look hopeless, and the second is strength when we feel like giving up.

Comfort is so important that God goes on record to say that He is the God of all comfort (2 Cor. 1:3). Then the apostle Paul makes some awesome statements about God, "who comforts us in all our affliction so that we may be able to comfort those who are in any affliction with the comfort with which we ourselves are comforted by God" (2 Cor. 1:4). What does comfort, defined as hope and strength, have to do with the difficulty to forgive? Notice the spectrum of God's comfort: "in all our affliction."

The word translated "affliction" (*thipsis*) means primarily a pressing or a squeezing pressure, usually from the outside. Affliction is like being squeezed in a vise. Our English word comes from the Latin, *afflicto*, "to strike on." Afflictions are crushing blows. They can be physical or emotional, resulting in a deep burden in our spirit. The Apostle John used this word to describe a woman's childbirth experience that is both physically and emotionally distressful (John 16:21).

Are afflictions that believers experience painful? Ask Paul. "For we do not want you to be unaware, brethren, of our affliction which came to us in Asia, that we were burdened excessively, beyond our strength, so that we despaired even of life" (2 Cor. 1:8). Repeated hurts, both physical and emotional, drained his strength and led to despair, even to the point that the hope of making it seemed dim.

Those who have sustained repeated offenses grow weak and feel hopeless. In this weakened state, the struggle to forgive is unfortunately given up.

I have had to nurse those with wounded hearts back to some degree of spiritual strength before doing major spiritual surgery. Forgiveness can be radical surgery for some.

Hopeless despair definitely makes forgiveness hard, if not impossible.

Vicky felt walled in with hopelessness. Her despair rolled over her like San Francisco fog as it comes in from the sea. It hugs the contour of the coastal hills, engulfing everything in its path. Soon you are in a dense, gray, damp world, scarcely able to see your extended hand.

Vicky was tired. Spent. Drained. She was going to need strength from the outside. God will do just that through personal encouragement of friends, His Word, and definitely by His Spirit in prayer.

"Vicky," I began slowly, "it sounds like you are carrying quite a load. Would you be open to share it with me?"

Often, just having a second party acknowledge their hurt gives them relief. Sometimes we are afraid to acknowledge another's hurt because we feel we would have to agree with it. True, the hurting person's response may be wrong, but acknowledging their hurt does not mean you think it is right. It just means you acknowledge from their perspective that they are hurting.

This is crucial. Failure to recognize a person's deep emotions, right or wrong, conveys to them that they can't trust you with the details. Instant judgment of another person's hurt may close the door on your opportunity to lead them to biblical healing.

Vicky's growing bitterness was dead wrong. It had to be addressed. Yet it took some compassionate understanding first. Trust sometimes has to come before truth is conveyed. Again, people may not care what you know until they know you care. Are you safe to open up to? If you are, you will be able to do for them what God's Spirit does; namely, guide them to the truth, not drive them to it (John 16:13).

Vicky's response to my offer was instant, "Do you have all day? Even then, we'll just get started. Never mind, you've heard it all before anyway."

She's right. There is not much new under the sun (Eccles. 1:9). No trial has overtaken any of us but such as is common to human experience in general (1 Cor. 10:13). The designs of life vary, but they are woven with some basic colors of thread.

She shared her story. Growing up, marriage, in-laws, and parents all figured prominently into her tapestry of hurts. But God arrested my attention with what might be one of the critical issues making it hard for her to continue forgiving.

"Vicky, you mentioned earlier that you are not going to try to forgive again. It didn't work for you. Those involved in your life keep hurting you."

"You got it. No more forgiveness stuff. It didn't work with them."

FORGIVENESS TAKES A BAD RAP

Through the years I've catalogued many reasons a person may find it hard to forgive. I was personally surprised to discover the list was not long. Vicky's reason rated as one of the top ten hindrances that cause believers to balk at forgiveness. She had misunderstandings about what forgiveness is and what it does or does not do. I probed Vicky further.

"When you think of forgiveness, what comes to your mind?"

"You just turn a person over to God for hurting you . . . release them yourself. That's it."

"Did you do that?"

"Yes."

"What didn't work?"

"Nothing got better. They just keep doing the same thing."

"What were you expecting?"

"Well, I did what I was supposed to. I just expected things to get better. They would just be different."

Vicky had two major issues that made it hard for her to forgive. First, she was confusing the fact of forgiveness with the fruit of forgiveness. As a result, the fact of forgiveness was taking a bum rap. Next, she did not realize there may be something within her control to greatly reduce others' perpetual offenses. She thought she was powerless, but we will see later she had the potential of being very powerful.

FACT OR FRUIT OF FORGIVENESS?

We discussed in the previous chapter the reality that many people confuse the actual act of forgiveness with the potential results of forgiveness:

"Forgiveness is a good feeling you have toward others."

"I can talk to them now."

"We seem to get along better."

"It doesn't hurt as badly as it did."

"I just don't think about it any more."

These are all the potential fruit of genuine forgiveness, but they are not forgiveness.

What confused Vicky was that she unknowingly felt that forgiving her immediate and extended family would in itself produce a new relationship with them. What really reinforces this is that sometimes it does happen. Bonnie witnessed this in a neighborhood conflict.

Bonnie had been working on plans for a neighborhood

block party. Others even offered to help. About the time she was going to produce the invitations, another invitation arrived in the mail. One of the neighbors decided to have the party sooner and unilaterally distributed invitations and invited Bonnie to the party.

That hurt. It was hard to attend and be cheerful. She finally forgave them, but they never owned up to their offense. Some neighbors wondered how Bonnie would respond to it. She worked it through with the Lord. She was free. She lived out the proverb that declares, "A man's discretion makes him slow to anger, and it is his glory to overlook a transgression" (Prov. 19:11). She was chipper. When she associated with the offending neighbors they, too, seemed more friendly. No one knows for sure why. But even God asserts that, "when a man's ways are pleasing to the Lord, He makes even his enemies to be at peace with him" (Prov. 16:7). This may have been the case. But this is not an absolute. Jesus pleased His Father and His enemies killed Him.

Often people respond to our changed attitude or cheerful countenance which is a result of our forgiving them. Vicky believed that forgiveness always resulted in things getting better. When it didn't, she blamed forgiveness itself. Jesus forgave those who were killing Him, and things did not get better for Him. Stephen forgave those who were stoning him, yet it did not stop the hail of rocks that ultimately killed him.

BUT THEY'LL JUST DO IT AGAIN

Vicky's logic ran in this vein, "I know I should forgive them, but they are just going to hurt me again, and I'll just have to forgive them again." You know something? She is right.

It reminded me of home. When I was a little boy, my mom had three dishwashers. They were all powered by "armstrong." There was my older brother, Carl, then myself, followed by my younger brother, John. We were all four years apart.

There were three phases in the washing cycle. One boy would clear the table. One would wash the dishes, and the other would have to dry them. I vividly recall proposing to my mother a brilliant idea. Why wash these dishes tonight? They'll only have to get washed again tomorrow night.

I have come to learn that a lot of life is repetition. Looking at my nicely mowed lawn brings a sense of satisfaction. But I know that in a week to ten days, I will have to mow it again. My nearly new home had quality paint on it. Five years later, I was having to touch it up because of the harsh Midwest winters.

Do I have to mention shaving, showering, vacuuming, dusting, trimming, washing, cooking, to say nothing of preventive maintenance? I love the smell of my freshly bathed grandchildren. But it seems that in no time they are having to be soaked again in the tub. Nothing on the human plane lasts forever. The second law of thermal dynamics guarantees things are going to wear down. Not to mention our household appliances that have planned obsolescence built-in.

I personally believe it is a way of God. Everything around us takes maintenance. Recently I saw some flaking "maintenance free" siding on a home. It is usually only maintenance free until it is paid for. But nothing is maintenance free when it comes to relationships. Offenses are going to happen. The need to do maintenance in relationships was the whole basis of the apostle John's first letter.

The most frequently quoted verse in First John is in chapter 1, verse 9: "If we confess our sins, He is faithful and righteous to forgive us our sins and to cleanse us from all unrighteousness."

Great verse. But verse 9 is preceded by verse 8, "If we say that we have no sin, we are deceiving ourselves, and the truth is not in us." Sin and offenses are inevitable. But in the context of this chapter the word "fellowship" is used four times. John clearly states his purpose for writing this letter was "that you also may have fellowship with us" (1 John 1:3). Sin impedes fellowship. It has to be forgiven, sometimes frequently, in order to maintain a relationship in fellowship. Now we run head long into the seventy-times-seven issue. What do I do when I keep getting hurt, especially by those closest to me? This was Vicky's dilemma.

490 CHEEKS

I remember a friend I had in high school who enjoyed a good fight. He was a Christian. I happened to mention to him what Jesus said to do when we get hit—turn the other cheek (Matt. 5:39). He looked me firmly in the eyes and stated tersely, he only had two cheeks. He was right anatomically, but he was wrong scripturally.

I was not quick enough to recall to him Jesus' response to Peter's question of how many times one would be obligated to forgive. Peter, attempting to answer his own question, generously suggested seven times. He may have known that traditional Rabbinical teaching stated that an offended brother only had to forgive three times. Peter doubled it and added one to make it a perfect number and a perfect response.

But Jesus was pointed in His response to Peter: "I do not say to you, up to seven times, but up to seventy times seven" (Matt. 18:22). That amounts to 490 "cheeks." But numerical limits were not what Jesus was attempting to convey. He explains this in a parable about a certain king who released and forgave a slave of an astronomical debt in the millions of dollars. Then that same slave refused to forgive a fellow slave of a debt amounting to less than twenty dollars (Matt. 18:21–35).

For years I used to think the amount of the two debts was the main focus. They are important. But Jesus is really teaching that forgiveness should be in direct proportion to the extent of the need for forgiveness. The king released and forgave all the debt. The slave should have forgiven all the debt of his fellow slave. Jesus then explained that since the slave failed to forgive his fellow slave all his debt, he would be turned over to the tormentors until he could repay all of the reinstated debt. "All" is the key word. There should be no limit set. It is not as important how much is forgiven as it is that whatever was owed must be forgiven.

We have had all our sin forgiven by God. We are in turn to forgive all the sin of those who offend us (Matt. 6:12). The focus is not on the number but on the thoroughness of the forgiveness.

Again, the elderly apostle John stated it clearly, "If we confess our sins, He is faithful and righteous to forgive us our sins and to cleanse us from all unrighteousness" (1 John 1:9). John knew offenses in relationships will reoccur. But confession and forgiveness continue the fellowship in the relationship.

SPEED BUMPS

Tom and Karen brought a very volatile mixture into their marriage. He was an alcoholic and she was a rageaholic.

Their marriage was characterized by violent verbal fights, slamming doors, and angry threats of divorce.

Through a national men's ministry, Tom was brought to the point of acknowledging he had never submitted his will to Christ as boss of his life. Major changes ensued in his life. Karen spent time identifying in depth the roots of her bitterness and released them all. It was like a mini revival blossomed between them. But conventional wisdom has taught me that this honeymoon is good, but not permanent.

In the past, their clashes could be compared to smashing a car into a brick wall at high speed. Lots of damage. I explained to them that they may not experience the same high degree of conflict as they had in the past, but that they would encounter what I call "speed bumps."

Karen and Tom would have conflicts. But with the reduction of excess baggage and with better communication skills, their conflicts would be more comparable to speed bumps in parking lots encouraging motorists to slow down—not high casualty brick walls. The worst they could lose is a muffler, not a life—let alone a marriage.

Then I suggested something Linda and I have done for years in our own marriage.

CLEAN PLATE

Karen was struggling with forgiving Tom for his periodic insensitivity, thoughtlessness, and blatant selfishness. He would finally come around and acknowledge his error. But she was growing weary of it.

"Karen, suppose you served Tom spaghetti Monday night for supper. Later you picked up his plate and laid it on the kitchen counter without washing it. Tuesday night you served him chicken fried steak with a rich creamy gravy on the same unwashed plate from the previous evening. Then, Wednesday evening you worked hard and made a full Chinese meal. His favorite. But you served it on the same unwashed plate from the previous two nights. Question. "Would you ever do such a thing as that?" Her shocked face said it all. Never in a million years.

"Why wash the plate if it is only going to get dirty again?"

"Fear of salmonella poisoning would prevent you from doing that."

The point was almost clear. I explained that they both have hurt each other deeply. Hurts will build up like food encrusted on those plates over the years. It took extreme measures to get them clean. The fact they are clean today does not mean they were never caked with unwashed food from the past. But now they are clean, washed after each meal, like hurts that are forgiven after every offense. Then I told them of our clean plate plan.

Linda and I planned a trip to Table Rock Lake. We had some household tasks to complete before we left. In our rush to finish and get going, we were impatient with each other and feelings were hurt.

The trip to the lake was quiet. Too quiet. After unpacking that evening we went for a walk along the lake shore. Linda quietly said, "I think I need a fresh start. I think we both do." We acknowledged our wrong responses and hugged each other as the dock lights danced on the rippling lake. We even laughed. You see, we had just finished taping our 26-week-long television series, *Fresh Start*. We needed a fresh start ourselves. We washed our emotional dishes. We began our three-day mini-vacation with a clean plate. But Vicky was tired of cleaning her family's plate.

THIS ONE'S FOR YOU

"Vicky, you are right. No amount of forgiveness is going to change those who have repeatedly hurt you. They may or may not appreciate how hard you have worked to maintain any semblance of a relationship. The greatest benefit from using the God-designed tool of forgiveness is for your benefit, not theirs." Vicky gave me the look that said, "I don't need it." But sadly enough, she did.

I have seen this expressed before. I saw it in Fred's eyes. Before Fred was willing to put his dad in the Jesus jail, he had to be convinced it was to his personal advantage to do so. Fred had been there. Vicky was now there. Vicky needed the rest of the unmerciful slave story to convince her to get back on track.

"Vicky, Jesus concluded his parable of the unforgiving slave by saying, 'And his lord, moved with anger, handed him over to the torturers until he should repay all that was owed him. So shall my Heavenly Father also do to you, if each of you does not forgive his brother from your heart'" (Matt. 18:34, 35).

Fred thought he had his dad in his prison. But he finally realized he was in his own prison of bitterness—and was being tormented night and day.

While waiting in airports, I have found myself watching people hurriedly walking by. From time to time my eyes will spot a kind of face I have seen before. The eyes are stern in sunken sockets. The lips are tight and turned down. The forehead is etched with deep wrinkled furrows. Bitterness made this face. This face reflects a life tortured by anger through the years.

I asked Vicky if she had ever seen such a face. She acknowledged me with her "who hasn't" look. I asked her a simple question. "Do you want that face?" No one ever says yes.

"Do you know how she got that face?"

"Being bitter all her life," came the terse reply.

"Do you think she ever intended to end up that way?"

"No."

After a pause, she responded in a reflective tone of voice, "I guess it was because she stopped washing the plate." She got it!

Forgiveness is primarily for our benefit. It does not usually stop, prevent, control, or change other people's behavior. It can influence, and on rare occasions, affect some change in others, but for the most part this discipline of life is for our benefit.

Vicky's first struggle that prevented her from continuing to forgive was the confusion that her forgiving spirit would change others. It didn't. We not only do it because it is right, but we also do it because it is right for us, for our benefit. She got it! But if I was to leave her at that point without addressing her second issue, it would be like leaving her stranded in the middle of a high traffic, four-lane highway. She needed to know how to walk to safety. She needed to understand there are appropriate biblical measures that could greatly reduce the frequency and intensity of future hurts.

SEPARATE BUT IMPORTANT

As I mentioned in chapter 1, a common thread has been woven throughout this book. Before these friends, whose stories I have shared with you, could forgive, a secondary issue had to be addressed. Sally could not use the biblical tool of forgiveness until she gave herself "permission" to admit her anger. Nancy found it hard to forgive because she felt forgiveness was the same as forgetting. Fred was bound and determined not to forgive until the revenge issue was addressed. Joy could not initially separate forgiveness and the personal identity issue. Andrew made it clear that he was not going to forgive his dad until he was able to see how he could relate to his dad if he forgave him.

Each of these friends had separate issues that made it hard for them to forgive. But these separate issues were equally important to them. Why? Simply because we are not single-issue creatures, but multi-issue creatures.

That was what was in store for Vicky. How would she deal with repeat offenses? This was the second issue that made it hard for her to forgive.

OVER AND OVER

Vicky worked through her wishful thinking that forgiveness of her parents would change them. That was the first issue that helped make continued forgiveness possible for her. But then she asked the question that was to unlock for her the second doorway to forgiveness and freedom.

"It never stops," Vicky began. "Sometimes it's okay, then there is a lull, and then something else happens. It just keeps happening over and over again. If I can't stop them from repeatedly hurting me, what can I do? I don't know if I can take this junk much longer."

One seeming disadvantage for Vicky was that I did not have access to her parents. It would have been ideal to have met with them, so that I could understand their needs and help get them met in a much healthier way. However, what was taking place with Vicky was more of the kind of reality that people-helpers face. Only one person was open for help, and Vicky was the one.

"Vicky, we have been talking somewhat in generalities as to what your parents keep doing to you. Would you list for me what they keep doing over and over that is so hurtful to you?"

Like a well-rehearsed prosecutor, summarizing the charges before the jury, Vicky began:

The other day my mom stopped by my house on her way to pick up Dad from his part-time job. I was making a cake for my husband Todd's birthday. She walked in the house without even knocking, barged into the kitchen—never said "hello" or "hi" but walked right up next to me by the kitchen counter—and said, "Looks like you're trying to make a cake. A box cake at that. You know you were never good at baking. I used to have to bail you out all the time. I told you, you should just buy one and not embarrass us all with a flop. I don't have much time, but I can see you need my help. You always did.

I shook like a child. I saw myself like a little girl—not the mother of teenagers and the wife that I am.

I have an older sister. She can do no wrong. I can do no right. Growing up I was repeatedly compared to her. "Why can't you be like your older sister?" was both my mother's and father's constant challenge to me.

We were close in age and could wear each other's clothes. She could freely help herself to my clothes, but she would whine to my parents if I touched hers. I was told to stop upsetting her. My folks never addressed the borrowing issue. I was called selfish or stingy for not sharing. I was told not to be a troublemaker by wearing her clothes.

Today, most all conversations with my mom on the phone are centered around my sister's kids, her house, her husband's job, just on and on. If I do call my mom, she shames me for not calling her sooner. Ironically, she never calls me unless she needs me to do something for her.

Mom, and my dad, too, use guilt to manipulate me into doing what they want, when they want: "I guess I will just have to call your sister. She is never too busy to help her mother." Ironically, my sister does nothing for them. I'm the one who normally drops everything for them.

I feel I was an unwanted child. I was usually ignored at home. I am ignored at family dinners. If I make a comment, insert an opinion, or make a suggestion, it may get met with a pause or a glance, but the conversation just continues. I can handle that, but my mom will phone me and ask my advice on something. Just like a fool, I respond, and she spends the next ten minutes letting me know how foolish it was and that I never made sense anyway.

I love my mom, but she is a control freak. She turns every conversation back to herself, even if you are talking about her grandkids.

Holidays are a dread, not a delight. She will call us to inform us where Thanksgiving dinner will be, who will bring what, and when. Just try to insert a preference, change, or suggestion and you are shamed for trying to mess things up. If that does not work, she will say, "Don't you think I know what I'm doing?" If we want to split the holidays with Todd's folks, she reminds me that she has always been there for us, and at least we owe her this.

It is not the purview of this book to thoroughly cover the issues adult children have with parents. But Vicky was adamant about not forgiving her parents. The following insights made a major difference in how she viewed herself in relationship to her parents. She never dreamed she had biblical options for dealing with her parents.

"HONOR" VERSUS "OBEY"

One of the biggest problems adult children have as it relates to their parents is that they fail to distinguish between honoring their parents and obeying them. As children, we are to do both (Eph. 6:1–3). We are to honor our parents for a lifetime, but we are not responsible to obey them after we are married.

God alerts us to the fact that our quality of life may depend on this continual honor, "That it may be well with you, and that you may live long on the earth" (v. 3).

I cannot recall meeting a person who had a biblically balanced life that did not have at the core of his belief system the quality of honor. Honor never ceases, but obedience to parents does.

From the beginning of the institution of marriage, a couple was to leave their father and mother and cleave to each other (Gen. 2:24). A precise order is established for a man and woman in marriage (Eph. 5:22–25). But what was hanging up Vicky was the thought that to obey God and honor her parents meant she had to do what her mother said. What Vicky failed to understand was that honoring parents is an attitude of the heart, not obedience to the capricious wishes of her parents (or even friends for that matter). As an adult you can respectfully say no. The three Hebrew young men respectfully informed King Nebuchadnezzar that they would not be bowing down to his golden idol (Dan. 3:18). They honored the king with respect, but obeyed God.

It became important for Vicky to understand that it is not dishonoring to her parents to graciously decline an invitation, a request (when unreasonable), or even a command. That was totally new thinking for Vicky. "But," she insisted, "my parents would blow up and I would never hear the end of it." So did Nebuchadnezzar. In fact, he "was filled with wrath, and his facial expression was altered," and he gave orders to "heat the furnace seven times more than it was usually heated" (Dan. 3:19). This leads us to the next important concept.

ULTIMATE HAPPINESS

No one, including adult children, is responsible for the ultimate happiness of their parents. Who is? God. When people structure their ultimate happiness around any person, place, or thing, they are setting themselves up for disappointment in life and a serious case of misery.

God has assumed the ultimate responsibility for our needs (Phil. 4:9). It is the presence of His Holy Spirit in our lives that brings ultimate love, joy, peace, patience, kindness, goodness, faithfulness, gentleness, and the very important relational tool of self-control (Gal. 5:22–23).

People will set up human support systems to avoid facing their responsibility to trust and depend upon God. It is sad to see older parents who did not develop a vibrant faith. For some, bitterness has taken its ultimate toll, and as the writer of Hebrews tell us, it causes a great deal of trouble, and poisons the lives of many (Heb. 12:15).

Parents are responsible for their responses in their older years as long as they have their mental faculties. Furthermore, no son or daughter is ultimately responsible to correct or make up for their parent's unmet childhood needs or unprocessed personal issues (bitterness, insecurity, fears, abuse). When it is appropriate, minister to their needs as you are able and they let you. Often, we are more willing to help, or get them help, than they are willing to receive it. But because we are their children, they may not honor us as adults and respond to our sincere help. Jesus experienced this with His own family and concluded, "A prophet is not without honor except in his home town, and in his own household" (Matt. 13:57).

It is heartbreaking to see the fruit of spiritual, mental, and even moral neglect in anyone's life, especially our parents' whom we deeply love. But it is important to remember as adult children we are not responsible to correct it. As in evangelism, we are to water and sow with His Word and our love and care, but God is ultimately responsible to effect the change (1 Cor. 3:7). True, as adult children, we are to see that our parents get the best of care when they can no longer care for themselves. If we do not do this, especially for those of our own household, God declares we have denied the faith, and are worse than an unbeliever (1 Tim. 5:8). Even Jesus, while hanging on the cross in excruciating pain, bleeding and dying for the sins of the world, commended the care of his dear mother into the hands of the apostle John (John 19:26–27). But how does all of this work in the real world you may ask?

BACK IN THE REAL WORLD

"Vicky, when your mother calls with next year's Thanksgiving plans, and you and Todd would prefer to share the holidays with both sets of parents alternately, here is a suggested response: 'Mom, thank you for your thoughtful invitation. This year we have been invited to Todd's home for dinner, and perhaps we could come over to your home Friday evening, or for a Sunday dinner.'"

"My mom would have a cow!" Vicky exclaimed.

"Who is responsible for your mom's response?"

"She is, but I have to live with it."

"If you shared this with a honoring heart, and even went the second mile and offered an alternative, and she reacts negatively, whose responsibility is that?"

Her blank look told me she was not familiar with Peter's reassuring words when faced with negative reactions for godly obedience, "For this [suffering] finds favor, if for the sake of conscience toward God a man bears up under sorrows when suffering unjustly" (1 Pet. 2:19). Usually this passage is referred to when one shares his faith and receives a negative response. However, it has a broader application, even in the context of the family.

Jesus alerted us to these potential family conflicts even when doing the right thing. Before He sent His disciples out to spread the good news of the kingdom, He wanted to alert them to something that could well happen in the family structure. His opening statement had to be unnerving: "Do not think that I came to bring peace on the earth; I did not come to bring peace, but a sword." Then He targeted where the sword may cut the sharpest: "For I came to set a man against his father, and a daughter against her mother, and a daughter-in-law against her mother-in-law; and a man's enemies will be the members of his household." Then he concluded, "He who loves father or mother more than Me is not worthy of Me; and he who loves son or daughter more than Me is not worthy of Me" (Matt. 10:34–37).

"That's in the Bible?" exclaimed Vicky.

"It's not that God does not want you to love and honor your parents. But when you do not 'leave and cleave' to your husband and are still controlled by your parents, you may be honoring them above your marriage. And that is contrary to the God-designed family order."

Many adult children cannot say no in an honorable way for fear of rejection. Decisions are based on what their parents think. They are not free to be led by God's Spirit but are controlled by the acceptance or rejection of their parents. What's the result? They say yes, but mean no, and become bitter and tired of forgiving or stop forgiving altogether. But even Jesus said, "Let your 'Yes' be 'Yes,' and your 'No,' 'No' (Matt. 5:37 NIV).

To the degree Vicky was able to come to know and believe in her heart who she is in Christ—totally accepted—to that same degree she could act and respond as a mature adult with her parents.

We went through many scenarios that Vicky encountered. Each time I asked her one, or all, of these questions:

1. Are you responsible to obey your parents in this situation?

2. Are you responding to them as a child or as an adult?

3. Are you taking responsibility for your parents' ultimate happiness?

4. Are you taking responsibility for your parents' responses?

5. Are you attempting to meet needs in their lives that only God can meet?

6. Are you making your decisions based upon their acceptance and rejection instead of what God would have you do?

She sat there stunned. Vicky had been in a prison of bitterness for years. She found it next to impossible to forgive. Why? She felt helpless and overwhelmed. Now she understood she had some choices. There were things she could do and ways to respond.

Now she realized that she could bury the hatchet (forgive) and appropriately distance herself from their repeated blows. Forgiving her parents did not mean she was obligated to put herself in emotional or physical danger, even with her own famiy.

Her parents got worse. They turned the other daughter against her, too. But because Vicky chose to get well, it only highlighted the unhealthy needs in her birth family.

Our prayer time of release lasted over twenty minutes. She was now ready to forgive and release her mom and dad totally. Do you know what was one of the surprising side effects? With the anger and bitterness gone, she found she had a greater love for them. She is reaching out to them in many creative ways she never dreamed she would. Not out of fear, but out of faith and freedom.

◊

For Anne, the repeated offenses by her mother was only one of her issues. She struggled with every aspect of forgiveness. Her story has become a pattern for others to work through the hindrances of forgiveness—especially when it is hard to forgive.

Chapter 13

"I Don't Know Where to Begin!"

Anne was raised in an alcoholic, abusive home, the third child of five. Her father was extremely strict, controlling, and harsh. As in most cases, alcoholics have a dual addiction. For him, it was alcohol and sex. He was both sexually and emotionally abusive, not only to Anne, but to her three sisters and one brother. Anne's mother was raised in a dysfunctional home as well. Her mother's childhood was the scene of bitter physical battles between her parents, much of which she witnessed. Her grandmother was involved in adultery, and this was a constant source of generational conflict.

As a result of all the abuse, Anne became food, alcohol, and drug dependent, while struggling with depression, anger, rage, rejection, abandonment, self-hatred, the incest, and a perfectionistic need to control. She had trusted Christ as her personal Savior nineteen years earlier but was still in severe emotional pain because of the damage done by her father. One of her turning points came after she read a book about processing the pain of incest (*A Door of Hope*, by Jan Frank). She read it three times before she came to see me. One of her lingering issues was the need she felt to confront her father about the childhood abuse.

Little did I know at the time that Anne's journey to forgiveness would become a pattern for helping others who knew they should forgive but found it hard . What I learned from Anne's struggle to forgive, I would like to pass on to you. Walk with me now along the rocky path from unforgiveness to freedom.

I. LET THEM TELL THEIR STORY

As Anne sat in my office feeling compelled to deal with her issues, she was nonetheless very anxious. Being overwhelmed by the sheer enormity of what was before her, she in exasperation said, "I don't know where to begin." Since her primary pain was from her relationship with her father, I asked her to start from her earliest beginnings and share "her story" with me. It was during this time I acknowledged and helped confirm, along with her, her pain (Prov. 18:13). This gave her permission to share without condemnation and premature correction. God makes it clear for every people-helper to be quick to listen, slow to speak, and slow to respond (James 1:19). It is the naive one who believes everything he hears, but the wise look well into a matter, attempting to discern what direction the person is going (Prov. 14:15).

As Anne became comfortable, and felt accepted and safe, she was able to go deeper, as she felt she needed to.

II. ACKNOWLEDGE THE ANGER

Most people are more than willing to declare blatantly that they are angry. However, those who have suppressed pain for so long have also suppressed the emotions of that pain—especially the anger. Some sincere Christians, like Sally in chapter 2, will not let themselves feel anger because, for them, it brings up strong self-condemnation. They believe that anger is wrong no matter what. They fail to remember that anger is just a notifier that something else is wrong and needs attention, just like the red light on the dashboard of the car.

Carol was angry at God. But her anger was a notifier that she needed to grow into acceptance of her multiple losses and adjust to them over time.

I acknowledged to Anne that it was a normal response to feel anger, and even rage. Rage is an emotional barometer that tells us how deep and intense our hurt is. Anne had no problem acknowledging the anger and rage because it had caused a great deal of problems in her marriage and family and could not be ignored. However, for some, anger is there, but it is veiled in irritability and frustration. Anger can come out in overt or passive ways, but in either form, it must be named for what it is—a cry for help and relief.

It is important to make a clear distinction here between acknowledging legitimate anger and condoning the wrong behavior expressed because of the anger. Anne indeed left a trail of offended people because of her anger. But the goal at this point was not only to help her acknowledge her anger, it was also important for her to see how it was manifesting itself, and what its roots were.

For Anne this was easy. But more emotionally controlled personalities may have a strong sense of denial or a reluctance to admit to themselves or others that anger is present. Sadly enough, I see this more in men who are more apt to hide emotionally.

III. IDENTIFY OBJECTS OF ANGER

As Anne's story unfolded it did not take long to see that there were not only many players in her story, but many offenses by each player. It was at this point that I asked her to list each of the characters in her real-life drama. I asked her to list, without hesitation or evaluation, the objects of her anger, and their specific offenses. Often it is easier to tell the story than it is to list the offenses that each person inflicted. But it is important to identify and list these offenses so that they can be forgiven specifically. Only then can a thorough release be achieved.

I did not have Anne describe the details of the incest. However, it was important for her to name the offense specifically. From experience I have found that when a counselee states the offenses in only general terms (e.g., an uncle acted inappropriately with me), that later there is still much denial of the events, and full freedom is only further delayed.

Then, I asked Anne to write out her list. This further underscored the reality of the offense and the depth to which the forgiveness had to go. I believe it is for this reason that God often adds to the forgiveness formula that it must be from the heart (Matt. 18:35). It must reflect the depth of the forgiveness—not just the depth of the emotions. Forgiveness is a function of the mind, activated by our will, and not our emotions. Emotions, or how we feel, should never be the sole basis for obedience. Writing out her story by journaling became another tool that helped Anne discover all of the offenses against her. Journaling acts like an X-ray. A physician may feel that a patient's arm is broken, but the X-ray confirms the fact, severity, exact location, and type. From this comes the prognosis. When I broke my arm, I thought it only needed a cast. However, when the orthopedic specialist showed me the X-rays, I found out otherwise. I was in surgery three days later. Likewise, it was while going over Anne's "X-ray" (journal) that we were able to fill out the list of offenders and objects of anger.

Before we went through her journal, we prayed "David's prayer" (Ps. 139:23–24), asking God's Spirit to reveal to Anne those who had hurt her and specifically what they had done. This aspect is important because it is ultimately God's responsibility to reveal the offenders. It is our responsibility to be willing to let God do it, and then to begin the forgiveness process.

I could see Anne was reluctant for everything to be revealed at once. This is probably because it might be too overwhelming, and because it might be too painful to re-feel those old emotions. I reminded her that God is the God of comfort, and He comforts us in any affliction (2 Cor. 1:4). Why does He do this? He does it, first, for our own personal benefit, and second, so that we may have the ability and resource to comfort others who are going through any affliction (2 Cor. 1:4).

It was important to let Anne express her anger appropriately at each offense. However, two cautions are needed here: First, I have never counseled anyone to take a punching bag, pretend it was their offender, and then take out their anger on the punching bag. The research on this procedure is mixed as to its benefits anyway. Our instruction from God is to let Him exact the necessary revenge, not for us to do it (Rom. 12:19). I have had many people tell me that they felt better after such physical expression of anger. And they probably did. But I doubt that the husband, wife, or children who were the recipients of that anger felt equally relieved.

The goal of forgiveness is not just to feel better, but to be obedient—regardless of our feelings. Unfortunately, those who "felt better" often had to repeat the process many times to regain the same feeling of release. Beating a punching bag while visualizing the offender you want to hurt is much different than just punching a bag to release tension and stress. Jogging, brisk walking, aerobics, golfing, playing handball, chopping wood, or mowing the lawn are all good exercises that reduce tension and stress and are very healthful. But simulating a battering, in my opinion, is never appropriate. The apostle John declared that hatred in the heart was equivalent to murder (1 John 3:15). How much more would this be true if that hatred is acted out, even in an artificial manner?

The second caution for the counselor is not to minimize the hurt that was expressed. The offenses that devastated the counselee may not seem so devastating to you. Remember, you are not doing the forgiving, nor are you the one that was hurt. But you must at least acknowledge that it was hurtful to them and leave the seriousness of it to them. Some of Anne's offenses would have crushed me almost beyond recovery. Others, I thought, were really no big deal. Again, I was not there, and I did not experience them. Nor did I have the same background for coping with emotional and physical abuse.

IV. PURPOSE TO FORGIVE

Anne had forgiven her father when she became a Christian nineteen years earlier, but the fear, anger, and rage continued. Well-intended friends and spiritual authorities in her life kept suggesting that perhaps she had not truly forgiven her father. She was urged to look deep inside for an unforgiving heart. She did this over and over again. She was led to believe that if she truly forgave her father she would forgive and forget. It was here that I explained why forgiveness was not forgetting and what purpose the continued memories were to serve. Once she realized that her memories had a purpose, her anger and rage began to diminish.

However, what Anne did not realize was that there were others, like her mother and siblings, that had hurt her and needed to be forgiven. I asked her to review for me what forgiveness meant from her perspective. It was hard for her to explain. Then, I shared with her that all sin needed to be paid for, and that Jesus had already paid for that sin through His death on the Cross (1 John 2:2). To help visualize this procedure, I shared the Jesus-jail concept with her, just as I had with Fred (chapter 4). We then took her list of objects of anger, and I led her in a prayer transferring each person, offense by offense, over to the Lord. Of course she had acknowledged His power and responsibility to exact punishment if necessary. But now she was willing to ask God to grant mercy, grace, and pardon for each one just as He had done for her.

Her list of offenders populated her Jesus jail. But there was one other person she felt needed to be there—Anne herself. She believed that it was one thing to grant forgiveness to others—that she was now ready to do. However, she also held the false belief that she needed to forgive herself, and therefore could not accept complete forgiveness in Christ. She had a sincere heart, but she rarely cut herself any slack. Not only did she have a long list of offenders, she had an equally long list of those she had offended. She felt she needed to be forgiven and had asked many to forgive her already.

We helped her complete the list. But a familiar misunderstanding reoccurred: "I can't forgive myself." Because she was so eager to learn, and to obey, it was a treat to explain what she needed to do. She did not need to forgive herself, but to affirm that she had already been forgiven by God. All she needed to do, therefore, was to receive His full forgiveness and live in the light of that truth, not in the vacillation of her emotions.

Anne had lived more out of her feelings than the reality of truth. In time she learned how to discipline her thoughts and make them obey the truth (2 Cor. 10:5). Feelings became subjected to the polygraph test of truth and left to mature in time. As they did, a deep inner hunger emerged. Dad was forgiven, yes. That part of the healing process was complete. But now the natural desire arose to have her father understand the emotional hurt he had inflicted, as Nancy had of her dad.

Anne had a good biblical background. She had been discipled well. But, as is often the case with in-depth Bible study, personal application is sometimes minimized while all the nuances of meaning of the passages are explored and added to an arsenal of accumulated knowledge. This left a hole in her understanding of God's Word that needed to be filled. This was not difficult to fill for Anne, however. All I needed to do was review the purpose of our great High Priest and remind her of His ability to feel our feelings (Heb. 2:17–18). When I did, a warm glow eased across her face. She connected, and she was released.

V. RECONCILIATION

For Anne, there was still some unfinished business. She did not want to confront her father and explain to him that she really did not care for him anymore. She had maintained perfunctory contact with her father and mother, calling, and sending cards, gifts, and letters. However, she did not want them in her life, and for good reasons. She felt they were not only destructive personally, but she feared they would hurt her children and be damaging role models just as Vicky had experienced. Besides being a rageaholic and a very large man, her dad was the town bully, and never thought twice about beating up people for no reason at all.

I gently asked her: "When are you going to deal with the pink elephant in the living room?" I was referring, of course, to her denial of the unfinished business of attempting reconciliation with her father.

For many, when forgiveness is granted by releasing the offender over to the Lord, a huge sense of relief is felt, and the matter is put to rest. The need to confront dissipates. For others, however, forgiving and confronting the offender about his offense are separate issues. They may be willing to forgive, but there is a felt need to also confront the offending person. I leave the choice up to the individual. My personal belief is that reconciliation through confrontation is the better of the two ways—unless there are some serious mitigating factors, such as personal harm, implication of others, or creation of an even bigger problem than is being solved.

Anne was led to confront her father. Clarifying the offenses helped sharpen her focus on the forgiveness she had already granted her father nineteen years earlier. Next, she wrote him a letter. She used the same pattern Amber did with her grandfather. First she expressed the positive things she appreciated about him. Then she explained that she was on a spiritual journey of further growth in Christ and had some unfinished business to clear up. She then shared the entire list of offenses for which she had forgiven him. She further explained that she was not asking for "payment" for his offenses (sins) against her, because Jesus had already paid for them. But she wanted to accomplish two things: first, she wanted him to know that the vow of silence had been broken. No longer was she responsible to keep the secret of incest for his protection. The secret of incest is usually the seed bed of its continued perpetration. In the incestuous family, everyone is sworn to secrecy, and it is the child's prescribed responsibility to protect the father or any family member from any pain. Anne was concerned that if he acknowledged his incest, it would result in his suicide. But understanding that godly sorrow is designed by God to lead to repentance (2 Cor. 7:10) freed her to continue.

The second purpose for her letter was restoration. Mutually rewarding relationships must be based on truth, not unspoken secrets (1 John 1:7–10). She wanted her father to appropriately acknowledge his sin and her gift of forgiveness, thus freeing him, so that they could have the wholesome relationship that they had never had.

The letter was written and sent. Understandably, fear completely controlled her while anxiously awaiting his response. Then it came. She could not open it. She froze. Trembling, she brought the unopened letter to my office and asked me to open it and read it aloud. Neither Anne nor I were prepared for what we read:

> Dear Anne, I am unable to understand how I could have committed these unspeakable acts. However, I know that I did and I admit these abominations. I can't tell you how terribly sorry I am, and I do not expect forgiveness from you . . . I accept the guilt solely, for you were an innocent

child. These past nineteen years have been a period of great remorse and acceptance of the kind of person I am. Anne, these appear to be simply words, but I would readily give my life for this never to have happened and caused such great pain to you. Your father.

When Anne shared her story on one of our weekly television programs, I asked her to share a caution with those who may consider undertaking the same task. Anne openly admitted that her father's repentant response was the exception, not the rule. Denial is usually the typical response. If denial is the usual response, then one may question the whole undertaking. There are at least two biblical reasons for it. First, as in witnessing, we do not know who is going to respond in faith and trust Christ to be their personal Savior. Our responsibility is to sow and water with the seed of the Word of God and trust Him for the "increase" (1 Cor. 3:6–9), or response to our efforts. Second, Jesus put the primary responsibility on the believer to initiate reconciliation—whether the believer was the offender (Matt. 5:23) or the offended (Matt. 18:15). God has given to all of us the ministry of reconciliation, based on our reconciliation with Him (2 Cor. 5:18). Anne could have let the proverbial sleeping dog lie, or not stirred up the pot. In reality, however, the sleeping dog was sick and the pot was a boiling cauldron.

Anne's journey of reconciliation became a catalyst for the whole family. Her brother checked into an alcoholic rehab center and there found the Lord. One other sister began her journey of reconciliation with Dad.

Some would seriously question attempting this reconciliation by mail. However, I wonder if we would have many of the epistles penned by Paul under the inspiration of the

Holy Spirit if Paul was limited only to a face-to-face encounter (Philemon). I personally prefer a person-to-person encounter, in most situations (Gal. 2:11). However, I leave the choice to the one who is doing it and must ultimately live with the decision.

VI. PREPARE FOR RECURRING MEMORIES

Anne and her physician-husband became our personal friends over the years. I have noticed that even after all of Anne's hard work, memories do return. Often I have had to do for Anne what the apostle Peter did for his Jewish readers: "I shall always be ready to remind you of these things, even though you already know them, and have been established in the truth which is present with you" (2 Pet. 1:12).

I encouraged Anne to welcome the memories that would come when she recalled what her father had done to her. I suggested that she remind herself that she put him in the Jesus jail, and that he is in God's hands. Finally, I encouraged her to grow in her acceptance of the continuing consequences of his sin, and use them to deepen her growth into Christlike character.

VII. PREPARE RESPONSES

Early in my ministry I naively believed that if I could lead someone either to grant or receive forgiveness, my job was finished and the healing was complete. What I failed to realize was that those who were "healed" still had to relate on various levels with the offenders or the offended. What I later had to come to grips with was that even if the ones I had ministered to had made a significant change, that may not have been the case with the others involved. Anne was a classic example of this. How was she to respond to her dad now, and how was she to respond to those who had to forgive her?

VIII. RESPOND TO THE OFFENDERS

There are at least two groups of offenders. First, there are those like Anne's dad who acknowledge their offense. Obviously, these are the easiest to deal with. However, it can still be an awkward situation. It is important here to remember that you have given the offender a gift of forgiveness. It is now time to slowly rebuild trust and mutual good will. As with our relationship with God, He forgives us and treats us like brothers, but it may take time to build or rebuild a relationship. Occasionally, a rebuilt human relationship is closer than it ever was. However, for most, it will never be as close as if the offenses had never taken place.

The second type of offenders are those who do not, or will not, admit they're wrong. These are a dime a dozen. They may shift the blame and make you feel that it was all your fault. Or they may say that it never happened and you just imagined it—just like Vicky's family did. In responding to these offenders, your choices are many. First, you can choose not to associate with them at all. If they are family, however, this is obviously not easy to do. I have strongly encouraged counselees in these circumstances to relate in a casual, courteous, and gracious manner—as long as no continued harm is present. You are not obligated, however, to share on any intimate basis.

For Anne, her dad readily repented. She now has a love for her dad that she never had before. She would like to have a dad-and-daughter talk, but another obstacle enters in, appearing frequently. Anne, like many other children, went to her mother at age ten to explain what her father had done. Her mother flatly denied it then. Later, she admitted it happened but continues to deny any responsibility for passively allowing it to continue. Today she still sabotages any effort Anne and her dad make to spend time together.

The depth of abuse that transpired in Anne's home rarely takes place without the mother knowing, or at least sensing that something is wrong. Often, what is not known factually is known intuitively by a woman. How is Anne to respond to her mother? She realizes she must respond in a respectful way, but she is not obligated to carry on an intimate relationship with her. Honor is always appropriate (Eph. 6:2–3), but permitting continued abuse is never appropriate. Honor is an attitude of the heart.

Although she is not obligated to share with her mother on an intimate basis, Anne is obligated to do a number of other things. First, she is to pray for her mom, as for others who have hurt her (Matt. 5:44). Next, she is to seek for creative ways to bless or benefit those who have hurt her (1 Cor. 4:12; 1 Pet. 3:9). Finally, she has to establish some new boundaries.

Boundaries are not the same as barriers. I played football in high school. We had chalk lines that served as boundaries to keep the game within certain perimeters. They kept the quarterback from running through the grandstands and sneaking up on our goal. Boundaries help the game function well. Anne had to set some boundaries, or limits, as to the kinds of behavior allowed in her home when her mother would visit. For example, her mother is fluent in profanity. Anne asked if she would refrain from its use in her home. Anne learned to deal with her mother on an adult-to-adult basis in all respects. As an adult she is to honor her mother, but she is not obligated to "obey" her (Gen. 2:24; Eph. 5:22). Anne could have established a perfunctory relationship with her mom by setting boundaries, or she could have chosen not to associate with her at all. Withdrawing would be an option in this case. Proverbs strongly suggests: "It is better to live in a desert land, than with a contentious and vexing woman" (Prov. 21:19). And even Jesus withdrew from His persecutors when possible (Matt. 12:14–15). Whatever course of action is chosen, it must always be Christlike.

IX. RESPOND TO THE OFFENDED

Anne had hurt a lot of people out of her own hurt. Many of them she was able to contact and ask forgiveness. Of these, there were at least three responses. First, there were those who accepted her apology and graciously received her, wanting the relationship to either be rebuilt or continued. Second, there were those who rejected the apology and wanted nothing more to do with her. Of the latter, she had to respect their decision and perhaps try again in time. Scripture explains that it is easier to scale a walled city than to win back an offended brother (Prov. 18:19). You can continue to throw ropes over the wall, hoping one will catch so that you can scale it and, in time, rebuild the relationship.

The third group forgave her, but kept bringing up the offense against her. Reminding the offender of his offense is wrong, but it still happens. One of the best ways to diffuse this situation is to quickly agree again that what you did was wrong, and then thank them for their forgiveness. However, if you slip into a defensive mode, reminding them of their forgiveness and their subsequent responsibility not to bring up the offense again, this only stirs up more conflict. I have never seen a defensive response produce a fruitful end. Jesus modeled what our response should be in these circumstances: ". . . while being reviled [i.e., verbally abused], He did not revile in return; while suffering [being physically abused], He uttered no threats [of revenge], but kept entrusting Himself to Him who judges righteously" (1 Pet. 2:23).

Sometimes a forgiven offense is brought up to test your response. The correct response, of course, is humility and a lack of defensiveness. Many a sail has the wind knocked out of it when there is no further argument or repeated defense on your part. It has been my experience that those who continue to seek revenge against us and attempt to manipulate with false guilt are usually still stuck in their own anger and bitterness. In such cases, it is now their problem and no longer ours. We must live in the forgiveness received from God, even if it was asked for but refused by man. Yes, we are to seek peace with all men. However, we must realize at the same time that we may never gain that peace with every man (Rom. 12:18).

IT WAS SO HARD TO FORGIVE

Anne comes closest to having worked through most every hindrance to forgiveness that I have encountered. She knew she should forgive, but it was hard for her. It was hard for others.

It was hard for Sally because she believed she was not even supposed to have the normal emotion of anger.

It was hard for Nancy because she knew all along she had to forgive, but she could not forget her dad's sin.

It was almost impossible for Fred because someone needed to pay for all his pain before he could bury the hatchet with his dad.

Nancy was temporarily stuck because it was hard to release a dad who did not understand, or feel, how he had hurt her.

It was difficult for Rochelle to forgive her dad if it meant acting like it never happened and exposing her own children to potential abuse.

Dan's physical and emotional scars were daily reminders of his abuse which made it hard to release his dad.

Shirley thought it was too good to be true that she did not need to forgive herself, but to live in the reality of God's forgiveness.

It was hard for Carol to come to closure of her son's death until she came to grips with her bitterness toward God and with the fact that He did not need to be forgiven but trusted.

Joy found it hard to give up her identity of bitterness and learn a new identity in Christ.

Andrew needed to know how to relate to his former "enemy", his dad, if he did forgive him.

Vicky recognized it was especially hard to keep forgiving when nothing changed and the offenses continued.

◊

All of these are real friends. Their stories are true. Today, I am richer for having known them and for having been asked to walk with them in their journey to forgiveness. Today, they are enjoying the fruit of their hard work. They identified and removed their obstacles to forgiveness. It is my prayer that they have helped you. And now, you will know what to say when you hear someone say, "I should forgive, but . . .".

OLD TESTAMENT

NEW TESTAMENT

Conference and Retreat Topics

Dr. Chuck Lynch

- **Bury the Hatchet in the Family** (common sense biblical help in dealing with conflict in the family, extended family, and blended family)

- **Freedom from Anger** (how to reduce anger in any relationship)

- **Hard to Forgive** (practical help in removing the major hindrances to forgiveness)

- **How to Be a Biblical People Helper** (lays a foundation for helping people work through their problems in living)

- **Men on the Grow** (how to face your most difficult challenges and be successful and blameless)

- **To Love and Cherish** (how to develop a mutually fulfilling marriage)

For conference and retreat information:

Living Foundation Ministries
611 R. D. Mize Road
Blue Springs, Missouri 64015
(816) 229-5000
FAX (816) 229-5056